Jenny Mon
5-12 91

MEETING GOD IN THE DARKNESS

ROBERT K. HUDNUT

MEETING GOD IN THE DARKNESS

ROBERT K. HUDNUT

Regal Books

A Division of GL Publications
Ventura, California, U.S.A.

Published by Regal Books
A Division of GL Publications
Ventura, California 93006
Printed in U.S.A.

The Scripture quotations in this publication are from the *RSV—Revised Standard Version* of the Bible, copyrighted 1946 and 1952 by the Division of Christian Education of the NCCC in the U.S.A., and used by permission.
Also quoted are:
KJV—King James Version.
TEV—from *Good News Bible,* The Bible in Today's English Version. Old Testament copyright © American Bible Society 1976. New Testament copyright © American Bible Society 1966, 1971, 1976. Used by permission.

Library of Congress Cataloging-in-Publication Data

Hudnut, Robert K.
   Meeting God in the darkness/Robert K. Hudnut.
   p.   cm.
   Includes bibliographical references.
   ISBN 0-8307-1382-4
   1. Consolation. 2. Christian life—Presbyterian authors. I. Title.
BV4905.2.H83   1989
248.4'851—dc20   89-36228
                                             CIP

1 2 3 4 5 6 7 8 9 10 / 91 90 89

Rights for publishing this book in other languages are contracted by Gospel Literature International (GLINT) foundation. GLINT also provides technical help for the adaptation, translation, and publishing of Bible study resources and books in scores of languages worldwide. For further information, contact GLINT, Post Office Box 488, Rosemead, California, 91770, U.S.A., or the publisher.

To Tom Kapacinskas

who has shown me
and many
that the dark night of the soul
can bring the morning light of God.

I will give you the treasures of darkness.

ISAIAH 45:3

It is a strange thing that I am trying to say, and for that reason I can scarcely explain myself in words. I think that ill fortune is of greater advantage to people than good fortune. . . . The honey . . . is sweeter when the mouth has tasted bitter things.

BOETHIUS, A.D. 524

It is only in his wounds that the risen Christ can be touched.

PASCAL

If the abstractness of modern society can be said to lead to a repression of all the emotions, certainly the most deeply repressed are those we call "negative." The "positive" emotions such as love or joy lend themselves to all kinds of sentimental caricatures in popular art, which are probably more damaging to the spirit than outright repression of such feelings would be.

But what love does not know the ache of fear, what joy is not tinged with regret? . . . Modern man is farther from the truth of his own emotions than the primitive. When we banish the shudder of fear, the rising of the hair of the flesh in dread, or the shiver of awe, we shall have lost the emotion of the holy altogether.

WILLIAM BARRETT, *IRRATIONAL MAN*

Contents

MEETING GOD IN THE DARKNESS

ROBERT K. HUDNUT

PREFACE

A woman told me she had read all the latest self-help books and many of the humanistic psychologists, but she still had her problems. There were a number of things going on in her life that she could not seem to shake, and she wondered what she could do.

I have found her experience duplicated by countless others. The self-help books do not always help. There is the nagging feeling that something is missing, that the self-help books, while full of well-intentioned advice, somehow fail to hit the mark. And people are often—not always, by any means—left in the same fix they were in when they embarked on their "self-improvement program."

I have benefitted, let me be the first to say, from every self-help book I have read. They are written with clarity and verve and are usually replete with ideas about how to live a more satisfying life. Still, I share the uneasiness of my friends, and it is that uneasiness which prompts me to offer this book—not as an antidote to the self-help books so much as a complement.

There is an entire dimension of life which the self-help books ignore. It is a dimension given by the negative emotions on which the self-help books thrive, an area of personality which many of us have not begun to explore but which is all along exploring *us*. Feelings of anger, resentment, depression, guilt, loss, pain, anxiety, inadequacy, insecurity, failure, fear and so on are invitations to a side of ourselves which we may have missed—precisely because we have tried to self-help our way *out* of anger, resentment, depression and all the other negative emotions which gambol in each of us.

One way to self-fulfillment is to view these negative emotions as sending important signals. What appear to be the demons of our lower nature may well be the angels of our higher, bringing us over into a dramatic new land of self-discovery. And it *is* dramatic, as people suffering from a "mid-life crisis" or depression or anxiety will tell you. It seems as though the world has swallowed up such people—when in reality they are being given a whole new world of self.

Now there are, of course, any number of ways in which this "brave new world" can be opened up. I have tried to elucidate one in this book, which is a sequel to *The Bootstrap Fallacy: What the Self-Help Books Don't Tell You*. In that book I suggested the premise upon which one could hold a dialogue with the self-help books. In this book are "handles" for dealing with our problems through the power of *negative* thinking, the centuries-old "negative way" to self-fulfillment. A health problem crops up, a problem with the boss, a difficulty at home that will not let up, a sudden feeling that the whole house of cards you have spent so long constructing is about to fall. What this book says is that the worst is bringing you the best—if you will let it. When you hit rock bottom, you hit rock.

PART I
THE DARKNESS

1
MY FRIEND

My friend is a good man. He is successful at work, active in community and church. IIe comes from a fine family, went to a choice college, lives in a select neighborhood. He supports his family, pays his bills, contributes to charity, has many friends.

But all is not well with my friend. He is in the darkest period of his life. He and his wife are at odds, and it seems fairly certain that they will divorce. He is still a good man. She is a good woman. But for some time now their lives have been enveloped in darkness.

My friend is everyman. His wife is everywoman. We all reach those points in our lives where what appeared to be together is actually falling apart. It could be your marriage, your job, your self-image. Some tragedy could have struck. You could be in an agony of grief or guilt or fear.

His wife and I talked. We talked every week for months. She took me into the darkness to search for the treasure, as he was to do later. The treasure was in herself. It was what we call God. It is God who comes to us when we have the courage to go into the night. And it is there that we meet the rest of who we are, the self that can come to light only in the dark.

My friend and I talked. I went to his office. He was enraged. "How could this happen to me?" he asked. It is the question of every man, every woman, into whose life the dark has come. It was the question of Job in the Bible, a good man, successful at work, with a wife and children.

"How could this happen to me?" is the first question from the dark. It illuminates a whole new side of life, one we would never have known if we had not asked the question. My friend slammed his desk drawer. Rage is an emotion from the dark, bearing its peculiar treasure. We do not discover the treasure for a while, but if we will stay with the emotion the treasure can be revealed. It is the essence of biblical faith that Isaiah's "treasures of darkness" *will* be revealed to us.

The buzzer on his intercom went off. "Yes?" he snapped. He did not mean it. His shortness with his secretary was the last thing he intended. But until its treasure is revealed the darkness tends to pervade everything we do. When you suddenly become ill, your illness is the only thing you can think of. When your best friend dies of cancer, you cannot even go to the grocery store without thinking of him or her.

A few days later I was with my friend again. He told me how bad business was and how he might have to leave his job and strike out, at his age, to look for another. Fear had set in, another siren from the dark. He was beginning to run the gamut of negative emotions. Indeed, on my next visit, he was wondering aloud what he had done wrong that his marriage should have gone bad. Fear, anger, guilt—a classic troika of darkness, but bearing the treasure of self-discovery, if we will wait them out until they signal God.

So I went back and back to my friend. It is a long process. The book of Job is forty-two chapters. Impatience sets in. We want the treasure before we have succumbed to the darkness. But it is not to be. "If [the vision] seem slow," said the prophet, "wait for it; it will surely come." (Hab. 2:3) We have to believe that. It is a matter of faith. This is why we call this a spiritual journey. The way into the dark is a pilgrimage.

We have been together now so many times I cannot count them all. Revelation rarely comes in flashes. It is argued that it did for Paul on the Damascus road, but that was only after years of darkness persecuting Christians. Only then could the troika do their work. The hours of night are long before they bring the day.

"How long must this go on?" my friend asked.

"As long as it has to," is the only reply.

"When must I remove my sword?" the just-converted William Penn asked George Fox, his Christian friend.

"When you are ready," Fox replied. When the darkness has done its work, then the treasure will be revealed.

One Sunday they were in church together, in their customary place, and she was crying. It was a sign that the darkness was doing its work. Although he was referring to something else, tears are "an outward and visible sign," in Augustine's phrase, "of an inward, invisible grace." He ought to know. Like Paul, he went through years of darkness before he "saw the light." "It is impossible," his mother's pastor said, "that the child of such prayers and tears should perish."

"I've cried, Bob," my friend once said to me, "for the first time since I was a kid." It is God speaking. Our defenses are down. We are terrified by the dark. We have no idea what is in store for us. "My tears have been my food day and night," wrote the psalmist (42:3). But it was a psalm. It is in the Bible. His tears were bringing him God. Augustine's "confessions" were written through his tears. No wonder he could speak of grace.

Another day, I dropped by to see him he was in high spirits. Things were going to work out. They had had a breakthrough. If they could both hold on now to what they had discovered about each other . . . . But it was not to be. Time proved that their emergence from darkness was premature. The darkness tricks us, as we will see in a later chapter. We think we see the light, but it is only a will-o'-the-wisp. And we know that is all it is because the darkness closes in again, and the treasure is not yet ours. "I have tried everything," he was to say later, "and nothing seems to work."

It was an important statement. If "Why did this happen to me?" begins our journey into the dark, "I have tried everything and nothing seems to work" begins our journey into the light. As we spiral down into the dark, we try everything to buoy ourselves. We turn to books. We turn to counselors. We turn to friends. We turn to work and "lose" ourselves in our jobs. While each of these may help, none seems finally to work. Relentlessly, we are thrown off our own devices and onto God. God is the name that comes to us, to paraphrase Edwin Arlington Robinson, when we realize that we cannot lead ourselves out of darkness.

For some, that discovery is a long time coming. We are

used to doing everything on our own, being in control, running our families and our jobs. That is why the darkness is necessary to bring the light. And that is why very often those who are most in control, like my friend, need the most darkness and need the darkness the most. That is why Job needed to experience anger, fear and guilt. Then he could experience God. *God* is the treasure revealed in the dark.

One day I went back to my friend. There was a Bible on his desk. It was remarkable. "I never really read it before," he said. "Now I read it every day." He pulled it to his chair and read a psalm. It was a treasure from darkness. Without the darkness, the treasure would not have been discovered.

"He calls me every day," my friend explained. "He suggests something in the Bible to read. He's told me he will either see or call me every day so long as this thing lasts. It's been three weeks now, and he hasn't missed a day yet." He is speaking of a friend from church who has had his share of darkness.

"My other friends almost never call. Only this one. And I hardly knew him before. He just asked me one day how I'd been, and I found myself telling him the whole story. That was when he said he'd be with me. As long as it took, he'd be with me."

We must have others with us. We cannot discover the treasures of darkness on our own. It is the sixteenth-century idea of the priesthood of all believers. Our job is to reveal God to one another, as Ananias did to Paul. When we share the darkness, we begin to see the light. They were being the church together. So were we.

The telephone rang. I left my friend's office so he could talk. When he was through he motioned me back. He took my hands, and we entered the dark together. We prayed.

His grip was immensely strong, and what he said was this: "Thank you, God, for getting my attention as you have. Thank you for showing me that good can come from bad and light from dark. Help me now to hang in there, since I do not yet see the light. Thank you for your Word, which will reveal it to me. Thank you for John," and he named his friend. "Thank you for Bob. Thank you for showing me that whatever happens, it will be all right."

At the door he gave me another strong handshake, and as I walked away I could not help wondering, "Is it I who am walking with him in his darkness or he who is walking with me in mine?" For whenever we are in touch with another's dark side, we find our own revealed. The treasure we sought for the other is the treasure we find for ourselves. It is a great mystery.

My friend has put me in touch with my need for the Bible, my need for prayer, my need for someone to walk through the darkness with me. He was enlightening me as much as I was enlightening him. He was opening the Bible for me, praying for me, walking with me. I know he would not view it that way, but it does not matter. What matters is God. God is slowly materializing in our times together, and in his times with our other friend. For the first time in my friend's life, God matters a great deal to him. God *is* what you have when you have nothing else. God is the treasure from darkness. And only from darkness? No. But perhaps most profoundly. Although a religious man, my friend had never before *experienced* God.

You ask, How is it now with my friend? The door to his desk no longer slams. He is rarely abrupt on the phone. He is not at the moment divorced, but the chances are that he will be. He is not "out of the woods" by any means. He is still "in the dark" about much that is happening to him. But at last the dark is bringing the light. He has moved from "Why did this happen to me?" to "I have tried everything and nothing seems to work" to "Whatever happens, it will be all right."

His whole other side is being revealed to him. He used to be strung tighter than a piano wire. Now he has long times of calm. He used to be domineering. Now he can let others be. No, not always. But often. And often enough to make a difference, a difference big enough that you can see.

If he had not gone into the dark, my friend would never have "seen the light." People would not brighten when they see him, as they do now. He would have been the same controlling, demanding guy who, when you hugged him, felt like a plywood board. But now all that is changing. The rest of who he is is coming into view. Some call it the second self. Some call it the reborn self. When I am with my friend, the name that comes to me is God. My friend is making a modern pilgrim's progress through the dark night of the soul. My friend is meeting God in the darkness.

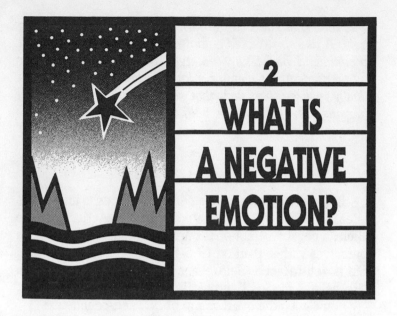

2
WHAT IS A NEGATIVE EMOTION?

She sat with her children at the front of the church. I did not know she was there. Someone told me. They were alone. It was the middle of the week. I went in to be with them. "It was a year ago today that Mom died," she said. "We just came in here to sit and be quiet and pray." I knelt before them and we held hands and prayed.

The emotion of her dying was on their faces. She had been in poor health for some time, but no one expected her to die. She was elderly, but again, no one thought she would die. She was that kind of person—enduring, always there, impossible to conceive of as not being there. So when she died it was particularly hard.

Her daughter wiped away her tears; and the children, one on either side of their mother, stared stolidly at me. It was then that she told me how they had all been getting help. A therapist would come to their home. She couldn't recommend him highly enough. It wasn't just for her mother's death; it was for a lot of other things, too. She finally realized, she said, that she couldn't handle it all on her own. She had to have help.

* * *

In a society that glorifies self-reliance, despair like this is easily classified as a negative emotion. Actually, in the Bible, a negative emotion is one which causes us to rely on ourselves rather than on God. It is an expression of sin. Sin is self-reliance. Self-reliance separates us from God. "To believe in God," wrote theologian Rudolf Bultmann, " . . . includes the overcoming of . . . self-confidence."[1]

Self-reliance in the Bible is characteristic of the fool. The Hebrew word for self-reliance means credulity, gullibility. It was used as a pejorative. "A fool will believe anything; smart people watch their step," says Proverbs (14:15, *TEV*). And "Do not rely on your own insight" (3:5).

Rise up, you women who are at
    ease, hear my voice;
you complacent daughters, give
    ear to my speech.
In little more than a year
    you will shudder, you complacent
        women;
for the vintage will fail,
    the fruit harvest will not come (Isa.
32:9,10).

There is, however, a positive side to negative emotions. They show us the folly of self-reliance. At first when we are in the grip of such an emotion, we pull out all the self-help stops. We talk about our problems. We read books about it. We "modify" our "behavior" so we can "deal" with it. We may end up in therapy.

We discover that our self-help measures, while admirable, are perhaps most helpful as necessary steps in overcoming self-confidence, for it soon becomes evident that none of our self-help measures ultimately works.

Each of these steps can be helpful, make no mistake. We get some relief. But often the negative emotion returns, and with increased rigor. It is then we discover that our self-help measures, while admirable, are perhaps most helpful as necessary steps in *overcoming* self-confidence, for it soon becomes evident that none of our self-help measures ultimately works.

Once we make that discovery, God can happen. As Blanche says in the arms of Mitch in Tennessee Williams's *Streetcar Named Desire*, "Sometimes there is God—so quickly." God is in the moment of self-discovery when we discover that self-reliance, while proximately helpful, is ultimately useless. It provides *No Exit*, in Sartre's famous phrase, from the negative emotion. God alone can do that. What the negative emotion has done, then, is first to separate us from God and, second, to return us to God. It is a remarkable tour de force for an emotion we had written off as "negative."

There are two kinds of negative emotions. One can destroy the self; the other can destroy others. Examples of the first are anxiety, guilt, depression, despair. Examples of the second are anger, lust, hatred—feelings which lead to violence and even war.

This book deals primarily with the first set of negative emotions, the intrapersonal. The dark night of the soul begins when I feel out of control of some area of my life and, being human, desperately try to regain control. It is this lunge toward control, toward recovering our emotional balance, that often precipitates our plunge into the darkness. It is in the dark night that we are met by the dark God, the "hidden" God of Isaiah (45:15), the God who is revealed in darkness.

This is not to say that God is not revealed in light. The positive emotions of love, joy, peace, patience, kindness, gentleness, self-control, which Paul enumerated in Galatians, are equally capable of revealing God (Gal. 5:22). But the God of light, of "positive" thinking, of "possibility" thinking and "positive mental attitude" has been systematically explored in our culture from Ralph Waldo Emerson to Norman Vincent Peale, and there is no need to duplicate their efforts. Indeed, the need now is to balance their efforts with those that reveal the riches of "negative" thinking and "negative" mental attitude—in Isaiah's phrase again, "the treasures of darkness."

In the dark night of the soul, the problem of the tension of opposites is resolved—but not solved. Hence the metaphor of night rather than light. When one experiences such darkness, one is experiencing the painful tension of opposites—night vs. day, dark vs. light, self vs. God, sin vs. salvation, doubt vs. faith. What one discovers in the dark night is that the negative emotion produces, or can produce, the revelation of a God within whom the opposites are contained—rather than a God within whom one of the opposites is absent. Indeed, God is what enables us to hold the tension rather than release it—either to idealism ("God's in his heaven, all's right with the world") or in what is commonly known as realism ("God's not in his heaven, all's wrong with the world").

It is precisely the letting go of the tension of opposites that causes so much mischief in the world, both intrapsychically and interpersonally. "If there is no God," says Ivan in Dostoevsky's *Brothers Karamazov*, "everything is permitted." That is the reductionism of realism.

What our negative emotions do is get us back in touch with reality. They plunge us into "the real world" where we really suffer with really bad feelings. They make it impossible for us to escape into the nirvana of Hegelian idealism. But they carry the distinct danger of plunging us into existential realism, what Kierkegaard called "the sickness unto death," despair. On the one hand, such emotions must not be denied. On the other, they must not be unduly affirmed. God is what enables us not to succumb to our negative emotions. God is what enables us to come to God because of them.

It is this coming to God that is the fascination of the negative. It is one thing to feel close to God at a wedding. It is quite another to feel close at a funeral, or in the days following. The first evokes gratitude, the second despair. And the question is whether the second will be the sickness unto death or unto life. On that question hang all the law and the prophets.

We are asked to feel our negative feelings deeply—if we want God. We are asked to go all the way with the self-reliance they engender—if we want God. Jesus was able to beat back the temptation to self-reliance in 40 days. It takes us a lifetime. His experience of greed, lust for power, and self-aggrandizement—all negative emotions—was necessary for Him to break through to God. It may astonish us to think that Jesus, too, had a dark night of the soul, but there it is. It is in all three of the earliest Gospels, absent only from the rationalist Alexandrian, John, who could not bear the "irrational" tension of opposites and so, throughout his Gospel, emphasizes Christ's divinity at the expense of His humanity.

What our negative emotions do is emphasize the divinity that is *in* our humanity. For we, too, are an incarnation. We, too, have devil and angel within. We, too, are tempted to violence and despair on the one hand and positive thinking which denies the reality of the negative on the other. Our negative emotions remind us of sin, but they also remind us of salvation. When we sin, we can be saved. If there is no sin, there is no salvation. Does this mean that we should sin, Paul asked, that grace may abound? Of course not. But it does mean that we *will* sin and therefore grace *can* abound. In fact, grace may well abound *only* as we experience fully the failure of all our attempts at self-reliance as the means of "dealing" with our negative emotions. Behind everyone's self-reliance lies a negative emotion. If we can just stay with our self-reliance long enough to watch it fail, then we can make it through to God. God can make it through to us. Indeed, God is what enables us to wait.

Times that call for "staying with" are what we call the dark night of the soul. Those who thus wait are what we call the church. The church are the people who stay with us in our dark nights. They are also those who share with us their dark nights. In this way we break through to the dark God together, two or three gathered in the name of the dark Son. It is best not to go through your dark night alone. You may never come out. The temptation to succumb is real. Kierkegaard died at forty. He had deliberately rejected the woman to whom he was engaged. Perhaps he wrote about "the sickness unto death" because, in his aloneness, he knew it so well. He felt his negative feeling, all right, but he felt it alone, and that made all the difference.

Note
1. R. Bultmann in G. Kittel, *Theological Dictionary of the New Testament* (Grand Rapids, MI: Eerdmans, 1968), vol. 6, p. 198.

3
THE
NEGATIVE WAY

The way to God through our negative emotions is a modern equivalent of the centuries-old "negative way" to experience God. Anger, fear, frustration, guilt, anxiety can be God speaking. It is a language we do not understand at first. How can God be speaking when you have just been fired? How can it be God when your child has died? When you have failed your final exam?

Our negative emotions are one way soul "matters"—that is, becomes material. Our positive emotions are another way soul "matters," but, as we have said, they have been dealt with by others. As we move through the "valley of the shadow" with our negative emotion, we suddenly "see the light." The spiritual begins to materialize out of the dark. Our days start to "brighten." The area of life that never meant much before now matters a great deal.

We all experience the dimension of self, which we call psychology. We all experience the dimension of others, which we call sociology. We all experience the dimension of the world around us, which we call ecology. But we do not all experience the dimension of God, which we call theology. Our negative emotions are one way to experience that fourth dimension. Life is too short, it might be argued, to live in only three. Samuel Gompers once defined labor's platform with one word: "more." We get more life with God than without. In terms of Pascal's famous wager, in which he decided to bet on the existence of God, we have everything to gain and nothing to lose by including God.

God is potentially included when the stomach knots and the chest constricts, when we have a hard time in the mirror, when there is havoc at night. No wonder the negative way has been called the dark night of the soul. You know you are in the grip of a negative emotion when you are unable to sleep.

The word "emotion" comes from the roots for "move" and "out." An emotion is a feeling trying to move out. It "wells up" and has to be "expressed." "Get it out," we say to someone in the grip of an emotion. This emergence is one's soul coming into view. Hence "psychology," from the Greek for "study of soul." The ancient Greeks spoke of the body as the "prison house" of the soul. They meant that when the body died the soul was released. But the soul can also be released when emotion is released, when it is so deeply felt that it is expressed, "pushed out." That is why, even in deep emotional pain, you will sometimes see people weep "tears of joy." Their tears are bringing their God.

God is said to be the principle of love, truth, beauty, and goodness at work in the world. But such a definition is too abstract. God is when I feel good about myself. God is when I am happy. That is not all God is, of course, but God is at least that. God is also when I feel bad about myself— but I don't *know* that until the bad feeling has been felt long

---

There is something about suffering, about the negative way, that attracts us to each other, binds us to God and acquaints us with our souls.

---

enough to bring God, as subsequent chapters will show. I feel good about myself when I have gone through my dark night of the soul, seen my self-confidence overcome and emerged into the "light of God's presence." Indeed, God is symbolized by light, as in haloes, and in Jesus, who is called the "light of the world."

To be sure, one can feel good about oneself as one builds one's self-confidence. Indeed, one should. This too is God—for the young person. But as we grow older, we learn soon enough that growth in self-confidence rarely equals growth in God. As we come up against those events of life before which self-confidence is helpless, we discover the need for a God beyond self-confidence, one who can make us feel good when self-confidence cannot. It is such a God, a more "mature" God, that can be progressively revealed as we go through the troubling events of our lives.

But isn't such a feel-good definition of God too simplistic? Perhaps. But perhaps the usual definitions of God are too complex. If God is not when I feel good about myself, then when *is* God? God is *When*, as well as *What*; an event, as well as a principle; a verb, as well as a noun. And how can I feel good about myself without having felt terrible about myself, as when I am facing death or divorce or job insecurity or pain from what someone has done to me or from what I have done to someone? How can I know the good until I have experienced the bad? How can I know light apart from dark? As we will see later, a thing is known by its opposite.

All the examples in this book are from real people with real problems. Curiously, they suggest all of us at one time or another. It is our negative emotions, among other things, which bind us to each other in our common humanity. Jesus was "a man of sorrows, and acquainted with grief" (Isa. 53:3). The most profound image we have of Him in the Bible, and the one most used by the first Christians, is that of the Suffering Servant. There is something about suffering, about the negative way, that attracts us to each other, binds us to God and acquaints us with our souls.

Soul is how God matters. Emotions are how soul matters. Thus soul is how God "moves out" into consciousness. Soul is the "inner light" we all have but which we are "in the dark" about until it is revealed by our negative emotions. A negative emotion *is* what reveals God—if, that is, we have "eyes to see" and "ears to hear," in Jesus' words. And all it takes to acquire eyes to see and ears to hear is to let our negative emotions be. Soul matters as negative emotions are allowed to emerge. No, that does not mean we are to "act out" all our negative emotions. That would land us in jail or psychiatry fast. What we are to do instead is acknowledge our negative emotion's existence. It is as simple as that. We are not to repress it. We are not even to suppress it. We are to express it—to ourselves. That is what happens alone in a chair in the living room during a dark night of the soul. It is how God makes an impression upon us.

The trouble is that our negative emotions are so powerful, so terrifying (the "fear" of God), that we want to deny them. Indeed, the word "negative" comes from the root for "deny." But denial is repression. Or we want to put our negative emotions off until we can "get around" to dealing with them. That is suppression. We are conscious of them, but the last thing we want to do is go alone into the living room. We do not want to face ourselves. And yet it is as the sea gull faces into the wind that it rides out the storm.

Expressing emotion is the key to unlocking the "treasures of darkness." Isaiah would not have used that phrase if he had not been expressing his soul, the deep, dark feelings that were enveloping his life. *As* he expressed them to himself, allowed them to emerge, move out, he created something indescribably beautiful, his book. As we allow our negative emotions to move out, we are at last in touch with the God who is touching us. God is coming into view.

God is pushing to be born in us. For many, God is what we are laboring at more than anything else in our lives. God is what is heaving into view as we groan with the burden of our negative emotions. Hannah appeared to be drunk with emotion. *Then* she broke through to God. Then God broke through to her. It was the same God who had been there *all along* for Hosea but whom he could not "see" until the veil had been lifted by the most profound crisis of his life. Moses killed a man. *Then* he experienced God. David had a man killed. *Then* he experienced God.

Paul had the Christians jailed, and voted for their executions. *Then* he experienced God. They are all astonishing examples of the negative way, which we tend to forget, to repress, to deny. The power of the negative is so great that it can easily turn in on itself and bury the treasures of darkness.

A man called to say he was okay with his wife and job at last. He gives the credit to God, who emerged after a mountain of self-help books didn't help—except, of course, to show him that he needed to look further for help, which was very helpful indeed. That is why I, for one, can say I have been helped by every self-help book I have read. A woman said that at last she had an idea of what she wanted to do with her life, thanks to God. Cliché? Perhaps. But clichés are clichés because they work.

These are people who got in touch with what was touching them through their negative emotions. They saw the light in the dark night of their souls. They had the courage to stay in their dark nights and find themselves moved beyond self-help. *Then* they heard the "still, small voice."

4

THE WAY
OF THE SOUL

She came to my office, but she did not stay long. She was *crying too much. Normally I would want to fix what was troubling her, but some instinct told me to hold off. She needed her tears. They were getting her in touch with what was touching her. As a man said, explaining something that was bothering him: "All you could do was love it." Paradoxical as it may seem, her tears were enabling her to love herself more than she ever had before.*

Therapy has been referred to as "the talking cure." The "client" or "patient" talks him- or herself into a deeper understanding of what the problem is and gradually, with the dawn of consciousness, feels better. It may

be, however, that when two people talk at a deep level it
is more a listening cure. The whole point seems to be to
get us to listen to what is going on deep within us. Her
tears were proof that she was listening and not running.
The very fact that she had come to someone else was also
proof that she wanted to "get to the bottom" of what was
troubling her. If I had rushed in too quickly, she would not
have heard what her deep self was saying to her surface
self.

"Words," the poet Rilke wrote, "are the last resort for
expressing what happens deep within ourselves." "Go to
your Bibles and listen," our Old Testament professor said
to us. "I look deep down," Starbuck says in Moby Dick,
"and do believe." Our tears are bearing us down. Or, if
you prefer, they are the negative emotion welling up. To
cut them off too soon is to prevent the darkness from
revealing its treasure.

* * *

So how do you do it? How do you get in touch with
your soul? How do your negative emotions move God up
and out and into view?

I

First, you let them be. You acknowledge them. You agree
to learn from them. You test the hypothesis that they are
revealing God. It is immensely instructive that the first
thing the disciples did with their negative emotions after
Jesus' execution was let them be. They "did" nothing in

the Upper Room other than acknowledge their grief, frustration and fear. The Bible uses the word "prayer" (Acts 1:14). And what is prayer but, among other things, letting our negative emotions be? "Wait, I say, on the Lord" (Ps. 27:14, *KJV*). That is how we gain knowledge of God.

Call, cry, sigh, groan, weep, pour out your soul—they were all words for "pray" in the Bible.[1] To be sure, so were rejoice, exult, make merry, praise, be cheerful, sing.[2] But remember, we are in touch with our positive emotions far more than our negative. Isaiah's "hidden God" removes the veil not only when we laugh but also when we cry. And it is in our cries, perhaps, that God is most revealed. Jesus acknowledged His negative emotions until "his sweat became like great drops of blood falling down upon the ground" (Luke 22:44). Jeremiah cries out: "Why is my pain unceasing,/ my wound incurable,/ refusing to be healed?" (Jer. 15:18). Job is in an agony of repression, then of suppression, as he refuses to let his negative emotions be. No wonder he exclaims:

> Oh, that I knew where I might find [God] . . . .
> Behold, I go forward, but he is not there;
> and backward, but I cannot perceive him;
> on the left hand I seek him, but I cannot behold him;
> I turn to the right hand, but I cannot see him
> (Job 23:3,8,9).

How do you know letting your emotions be is going to produce God? You don't. Remember, this is your hypothesis, your gamble. Moses longs for the Promised Land and does not make it (Num. 20:12). David is in anguish over his child and the child dies (2 Sam. 12:15-23). Rachel

weeps for her children, for they will never be seen again
(Jer. 31:15). Jeremiah lets his negative emotions be and
gets a question rather than an answer (Jer. 12:5). Even
Jesus in His cry of despair from the Cross dies with an
agonizing question about how God fits in (Matt. 27:46).
There is no "blessed assurance" that our negative emotions will produce God. But that is no reason to discard the
hypothesis. An hypothesis by definition is "an assertion
subject to proof." If it had already been proven it would not
be an hypothesis.

The encouraging thing about the negative way, however, is that its ability to produce—more accurately,
educe—God is constantly being demonstrated. That is
why Jesus could say: "Whatever you ask in prayer, believe
that you receive it, and you will" (Mark 11:24). And He
said it at precisely the time His own negative emotions
were building up to the supreme crisis of His life, as He
entered Jerusalem on His way to certain death. "The distinctive feature of early Christian prayer," writes an
expert, "is the certainty of being heard."[3] The first Christians' certainty stemmed from their intimate relationship
with God, so intimate that Jesus used the word *Abba*—
"Dad"—to describe it. God *is* who is there when I express
my negative emotions in my living room.

Here is how it works. We move from speaking to listening. We find ourselves *being* moved. That *is* God. This
is not all God is, but God is at least that. In scientific language, we move from beta to alpha, from twenty brain
waves a second, in which we are speaking, to fifteen brain
waves a second, in which we are listening. Our eyes close.
We breathe deeply. We wait. "I will wait for the Lord."
(Isa. 8:17). Isaiah knew this was the only way to garner
the treasures of darkness. As we wait, the images come.
They are God speaking.

II

Another way to let our emotions be is to give our dreams equal play with our thoughts. Conscious anxiety, for instance, is buoyed by unconscious fear. If we are to experience God, and as modern pilgrims progress rather than regress through the dark night of the soul, we must let the causative fear move out as well as the symptomatic anxiety. One of the best ways to do that is to employ a device rarely used to unearth the treasures of darkness—our dreams.

The Judeo-Christian faith begins not only in a theft, with Jacob stealing his brother's inheritance; it begins also in a dream, first at Bethel with Jacob's ladder and later at the Jabbok with the lonely wrestler. [4]

The key to unlocking the soul is to treat our unconscious life of dreams as seriously as we treat our conscious life of thoughts. It is a matter of equality, of balance, of giving the undiscovered parts of ourselves as much visibility as the discovered. According to the latest scientific data, we all have three to five dreams a night, and they can easily be remembered if we will simply practice the modest expedient of writing them down.

Our dreams are our inner family, and the idea is to befriend them, as we do our own family. Indeed, we can even share our dreams with those we love over the breakfast table or over a cup of coffee. Surely this is as enriching an experience, someone has said, as reading the Shredded Wheat box. It shows our loved ones that we value the unconscious, that we treat it equally with the conscious, that we are sensitive to God's emerging from within. I am sick, wounded, drowning. I am a child, a woman, a criminal. I am on top of the world, pursued, flying. I am locked in a lonely struggle on the banks of my personal Jabbok.

Dreams are the bridges thrown down every night between the inner and the outer self, between the unconscious and the conscious, between the self and the ego, between God and me. Therefore not to cross them in the light of the dawn is folly at best and, as we have seen, theft at worse. Indeed, before his Antagonist leaves, the protagonist, Jacob, asks Him to bless him. We are blessed by our dreams. They are the hidden God emerging.

III

A final way to let our negative emotions be and thus let God emerge is to refrain from acting them out. It is to treat *others* equally, not as inferior. The temptation when one is in the grip of a negative emotion is to take it out on someone else, to project it rather than introject it. But there is a moral quality to a modern pilgrim's progress that will not let us do that. Let the other be. Till your own garden. Tend your own compost. Do not dump it on somebody else.

This is what Jacob did not do. He acted out his shadow, tricked his brother out of his birthright, stole his inheritance. Even on the other side of his titanic struggle he is still the trickster. He says he will follow his brother south. Instead he gives him the slip and follows his own vision west. Fortunately, this is the last of his games, of playing out on others what he should have been playing in.

The change was a matter of time as much as anything. Just as we take time for our negative emotions and the dreams underneath them, so time was taken in Jacob's psyche to turn him from trickster into patriarch. It was twenty years later that he and his brother were being united. He was being united with his brother within as well as his brother without. He was around mid-life, the time when the self is eager for more knowledge of itself, when the sun of its achievements has begun to set, the moon of approaching darkness has begun to rise, and the moral container of guilt has forced the self to live things in as images rather than act them out as thefts.

*W*hen I accept the dark parts of myself as my own, when I "own" them, in the jargon of the pop psychologists, then I can accept the dark parts of others.

Instead of acting out the negative way with our moods and angers, we should instead be living it in. That is why we say, "I take it back," when we have said something to hurt someone. We realize that we have taken out on the other what we should have taken in to ourselves. Because we are unable or unwilling to treat our negative emotions equally with our positive, we refuse to treat someone else equally. That is how perverse the denial inherent in our negative emotions can be. Virtually all our ethical problems come from not treating others as equal. In discussing Israel and Palestine, Anthony Lewis of the *New York Times* writes: "The root of the problem, as always in the divisions of race and religion, is the refusal to grant equal humanity to others."[5]

When I accept the dark parts of myself as my own, when I "own" them, in the jargon of the pop psychologists, then I can accept the dark parts of others. When I am "together," when I am in harmony with myself, then I can love my neighbor "as myself" (see Luke 10:27). Then I can love the "least of these, my [friends]" (see Matt.

25:40) because I love my negative as well as my positive self and the "least" of me within me.

No, it is not easy. A modern pilgrim's progress is as difficult as any pilgrim's ever was. That is the way of the soul. On Valentine's Day we draw our hearts with arrows through them. Love comes with an arrow for Cupid. It comes with a cross for Christ. It comes with a limp for Jacob. It comes with hurt for all of us. And the hurt is that our morality, our love, contains our desire to act out our dark night of the soul, forcing us to internalize our negative emotions and thus make *soul*, rather than externalize them and thus make *enemies*.

At the same time, however, our negative emotions bind us ineluctably to each other. Jacob's name is changed to Israel, "God strives," and Israel becomes a nation and a race. He is every one. God is striving, through our negative emotions and the dreams and images and, yes, enemies they inspire, to be born again. God is our progress through the dark night of the soul.

Notes
1. J. Herrmann in G. Kittel, *Theological Dictionary of the New Testament* (Grand Rapids, MI.: Eerdmans, 1964), vol. 2, p. 785.
2. Idem.
3. H. Greeven in G. Kittel, op. cit., p. 803.
4. That Jacob's struggle is a dream, see S. R. Driver, "Genesis," in *Westminster Commentaries* (London: Methuen, 1954), p. 297.
5. Quoted in *Chicago Tribune*, November 9, 1979.

5

THE IMITATION
OF CHRIST

Let's get even more specific about how negative emotions are the way soul matters. What do you actually do with the negative emotion when it comes? Granted you let it be. Granted you give it its due as much as any positive emotion. What happens next?

I

You name it. "What is your name?" the Man in the night asks Jacob (Gen. 32:27). It is not always easy to name what is troubling us. A young man came home talking about a possible promotion.[1] In his excitement he accidentally knocked a china dish off the table. His wife flew into a rage and ran out of the room in tears. Instead of leaving it at that, she tried to identify what had upset her. She acknowledged her emotion and tried to gain knowledge from it. What she discovered was that her rage was not anger with her husband. It was not anger over the broken dish. It was not jealousy. Rather it was the feeling of being left behind. She knew that's what it was because relief flooded her body when she made the identification. That recognition was potentially a first step toward God.

Our spiritual task is to wait for the name to come, for the darkness to yield its treasure. If we wait long enough, the name may well be God. Not always, of course, but often, and often enough to confirm the way of the spirit for the modern pilgrim. "I have seen God," Jacob says (Gen. 32:30). He wrestles through an entire night, struggling to come up with the name for what is troubling him. As the dawn breaks and the Man leaves and relief floods Jacob's body, he realizes that what he has been struggling with is not just guilt over what he has done to his brother. He has been struggling with God. God has been struggling to be "born" in Jacob. The negative emotion is the emergent God. For twenty years Jacob had denied not only his guilt, which any pop psychologist could have told him; he had denied his God, which few if any pop psychologists would have told him.

"What is your name?" the Man asks Jacob, in an ironic twist. Jacob is being named *as* he names what is happening to him. He is achieving his true identity. He is going through his personal Gethsemane. His struggle is what is being asked of him. This is the negative way.

The imitation of Christ does not mean that we are to copy Jesus' life, which is impossible. It means that we are to emulate His use of the negative way. The Cross "contains the truth that the soul is moved most profoundly by images that are disfigured, unnatural, and in pain."[2] As we follow the "way of the cross," God comes. We become who we were meant to be. We are identified.

Just as Psyche in the ancient myth sought to discover the identity of her mysterious lover, Cupid, so our psyche needs to personify. "She" needs to name.[3] Naming is the essence of psychology. According to the ancients, when we name what is troubling us we have power over it. But Jacob, in the ironic twist, is himself overpowered and is himself named. This is how God emerges. We feel we are "out of control," in the hands of "a higher power." At the same time, we feel we are "more ourselves" than we have ever been. The demon of negative emotion becomes the angel of God. The modern pilgrim is transfigured. As we name our negative emotions, we live up to our names, to all that is in us. It is how God comes. It is how soul matters. It is how a modern pilgrim makes his or her spiritual progress.

II

Next, you embrace your negative emotion. The point of the naming is to get to know what is troubling us, and when we know it we can embrace it. The job of the ego is to embrace the negative presences within. Such a "descent to the cross" is the best thing that could happen to the ego—if, that is, it wants to be on a spiritual journey. If it does not want to be on a spiritual journey it may very well reject the negative emotion by projecting it, as the woman did with the broken dish, or by misnaming it "erroneous."

Embrace your panic. Do not project it. Jacob "was left alone" (Gen. 32:24). When our breathing constricts and our stomachs knot, we panic. Our panics are necessary to the appearance of God. That is why Mary is afraid when the angel comes announcing the birth of God (Luke 1:29,30). We have a moral obligation to love our panics, to talk to them, to turn the wrestler's hold into an embrace, to ask our negative emotions to bless us. "I will not let you go," Jacob says to the One he is embracing, "unless you bless me" (Gen. 32:26). We are blessed as we embrace our panics, rather than denying them by calling them "erroneous" or hiding from them as Adam and Eve did in paradise (Gen. 3:8).

We embrace the God who is embracing us. The healing dream in ancient times required being touched by the god. [4] Jacob is touched and forever after will limp. He is wounded, "crucified." *In his wound is his healing.* He is being made "whole," the root for "heal." We remain in the embrace of our suffering. It is the imitation of Christ. It is drinking the cup fully, moving from Eden to Gethsemane, and saying it is my cup.

We pay high tuition to go to school in this part of our souls. But this is what is meant by "living authentically." You are not a textbook person but a real one. Jacob with the limp, the wound, is more "real" than Jacob without. He can at last "feel good about himself"—not because he is without a wound but because "I have seen *God*" (Gen. 32:30). [5]

Embracing the negative emotion is how we can say we make progress in our emotional crisis. The word "crisis" comes from the root for "turning point." We are at a crossroad, a turning point. We can embrace or deny. If we embrace, it means we are viewing the crisis as a gift, which is the meaning of the word "grace" in the New Testament. Our emotional crisis is a gift, breaking the soul free from its identification with the ego.

Such liberation is why Jacob gets a new name, and why he is changed in the process. When you are "named" at baptism you are launched on your spiritual journey. From now on, at least in theory, you will view your negative emotions as gifts bringing you to God. You understand your crisis because you "stand under" it rather than view yourself as "on top of it." You are alone in the bedroom in tears, a symbol of drowning, "going under." But it is your soul realizing, becoming real. The submerged ego embraces the emergent God.

Another way to say "embrace" is to "mull." For Mary it was "ponder" (Luke 2:19). Maybe "consider" would do it; and considering takes time, as a good embrace. Maybe "cook" would be good. Or "simmer." When we embrace a negative emotion that has plunged us into a crisis, we let it simmer to the point where we can digest it. All the crises of our lives are still simmering, still being digested, still making soul-food.

Psychotherapy is the process of giving someone who has been wounded the space and time to mull. It is letting the images simmer. The Greek word from which we derive the term "therapist" meant one who served the gods.[6] The word came from the root for attend or care for, not treat.[7] Therapy is not treatment. It is imagination. It is embracing someone so that that person's images can come. It is caring for someone so much that you will not let that person deny the value of his or her negative emotions. Therapy is the priesthood of all believers. It is an imaginative ritual relating us to the God who is within us. Therefore it is therapy which goes on in churches, if they really are churches, if they are communities where people who limp, who have been critically wounded, embrace one another. And in the embrace the images come, the names. And the most authentic name is God.

III

Third, you release your negative emotion. Name it, embrace it, release it—this is the therapeutic process, the way we care for each other and ourselves, the way we serve one another. The Wrestler said, "Let me go, for the day is breaking" (Gen. 32:26). If a night-demon were to be discovered by the sun, his power would be gone. It was the ancient way of saying that we often feel better in the morning when we are in the grip of a negative emotion. With the coming of the dawn the nightly struggle is over, at least for a while. Remember, these are the treasures of darkness. This is the dark night of the soul.

*E*motional problems are not meant to be solved. They are meant to be used—for soul-making.

It is perhaps hard to imagine how releasing fits in with embracing. It is hard to rationalize. We have to do a lot of stewing before the flavor is released. "I go to prepare a place for you," Jesus said (John 14:2). They wanted to keep Him—but they had to let Him go. When He was transfigured and they heard His name being changed to "Son," Peter wanted to make a booth to hold the moment—but they had to let Him go (Mark 9:2-8). Later, when Peter named Him as "the Christ, the Son of the living God," Jesus told them He had to go, at the very moment they wanted most to embrace Him (Matt. 16:13-23).

We name our children. We embrace them for a while. We let them go. Let your negative emotion be. Then let your negative emotion go. Do you remember when we were children the little sailboats with their tiny sails that we used to float out on the waters? We would give them a push and let them go and watch them career in the wind and founder and wonder if they would ever come back. Release what is troubling you. Float it out on the waters.

Of course the little boats came back. What troubles us will come back, too. Emotional problems are not meant to be solved. They are meant to be used—for soul-making. But there is this sense in which we have to release what has panicked us. Jacob let his demon go. We do not hold our negative emotion forever. We let it go. It will be back, yes, because we do not repress it. But we also have to let it go. The stew is most useful when it is out of the pot.

"I have seen God," Jacob says (Gen. 32:30). He sees God in the process of naming, embracing and releasing. "Now is my soul troubled," Jesus says as He names His fear upon entering Jerusalem (John 12:27). "And what shall I say? 'Father, save me from this hour'? No, for this purpose I have come to this hour. Father, glorify thy name" (John 12:27,28).

Whatever your negative emotion, it can bring you to God. It is the way of the soul. It is the negative way, the road map for the pilgrim's progress.

Notes
1. E. Gandlin, cited in *Chicago Tribune*, January 3, 1980.
2. J. Hillman, *Re-visioning Psychology* (New York: Harper, 1975), p. 95.
3. Psyche was a maiden so beautiful that Venus became jealous of her.
4. Hillman, op. cit., p. 34.
5. All italicized words in scriptural statements used in this book are the author's and are used to emphasize and clarify certain ideas and concepts.
6. Hillman, op. cit., p. 192.
7. Ibid., p. 74.

PART II
THE TREASURES

THE TREASURES OF CONFUSION

6
THE GIFT
OF CONFLICT

She came to me in enormous conflict with herself. On the one hand, she wanted to stay with her husband and make a go of it. On the other hand, she had had enough. She had been trying for years, and nothing seemed to work. She was willing to work with me. She was willing to go to another counselor. But whenever they had begun counseling, her husband would last for only a few sessions. Just when they were beginning to get somewhere, he would drop out. It was unbearably frustrating to her, and now that the marriage was obviously not going anywhere, she had a decision to make. Should she be faithful to her marriage vows, or should she be faithful to herself? The two choices seemed to be in irreconcilable conflict.

* * *

Have you ever felt yourself in conflict between who you are and who you want to be? Have you ever felt tempted to stay with what you are doing and put off what you know you could or should be doing? The apostle Paul felt the tug of war so acutely he put it this way: "I delight in the law of God, in my inmost self, but I see . . . another law at war with the law of my mind" (Rom. 7:22-23).

I

When we speak of our inmost self, we are speaking of the deep, hidden self we are not in touch with but which is reaching out to us. It comes to us in the darkness, our dark nights in dreams, and our dark emotions. We have no control over this inmost self. It comes to us; we do not come to it. Suddenly we are paralyzed by fear, anger, guilt, depression. This is a harbinger of our inmost self. We feel we have hit rock bottom; then we reach our inmost self.

Whenever you are in the grip of a complex, whenever things are not working out for you, whenever you feel yourself overcome by one of your emotions, it is your whole self in touch with your partial. To view the neurosis as a symptom of pathology is to miss the point. It is rather a symbol of potential wholeness, completeness, of the self longing for itself.

Many, as Paul, recognize the presence of God in our inmost self, which we can grasp, or more accurately, which we can be grasped by—because the inmost self operates on us rather than we on it. We are passive; it is active. Its job is to bring God into view, to reveal the treasures of darkness. Thus what may appear to be the symptom of pathology is rather the symbol of theology. Our negative emotions are not symptoms to be cured but symbols to unite us to God.

Our job, then, is to take such symbols seriously. They are a compensation device for something one-sided in our personality. That is to say, they are showing us what is missing in our lives. They are revealing the rest of who we are and thus preventing a disastrous imbalance, which could permanently upset us. Indeed, it is precisely what threatens to upset us that is giving us our vision of wholeness.

Consequently, a dream is far more than a symptom of something that went wrong in childhood, a childhood trauma repressed, as understood by Freud. A dream is a symbol of what you are avoiding *now*. It is an attempt to balance your unbalanced life. That is why the Bible speaks so often of the fear of God. People avoid God. They are afraid of God. They do not want to deal with the rest of who they are. Not everyone has the courage of Abraham to go on a long journey into self. When Moses led the people out of Egypt, they, too, as Freud, looked back: "Is not this what we said to you in Egypt, 'Let us alone and let us serve the Egyptians'? For it would have been better for us to serve the Egyptians than to die in the wilderness" (Exod. 14:12).

It is these symbols, coming to us in our dreams and dark emotions, that, in the root meaning of the word *symbol*, "throw [us] with" the universal symbols collected in such places as the Bible and thus help us become what we were meant to be. When we take a journey, it is Abraham's journey. When we are afraid, it is the Israelites who are afraid. When we suffer at the hands of a nightmare or trauma, it is the Suffering Servant who suffers with us. "I complete what is lacking in Christ's afflictions," Paul wrote (Col. 1:24). His own suffering was the way he, Paul, became complete, whole, balanced.

But balance comes only when we are ready. The first half of life is given over to strengthening the ego. We get our grades. We advance in our jobs. We establish family and friends. The second half of life is, or at least should be—note the tug of war—given over to strengthening the life of the unconscious. It is no accident that Abraham is seventy-five years old when he leaves on his journey. In terms of his biblical length of years—175—that means 43 percent of his life is over. It is toward the second half of life that we want contact with the objective, suprapersonal side of ourselves, the side that will outlast us, that will beat death, the inmost self, God. That is why churches are often filled with older people. The exciting thing, of course, is to see churches filled with younger people, too, who realize early on that they are incomplete, unbalanced, and so are working on their integrity—their wholeness— even before they reach mid-life.

II

It is at this point of balance, however, that problems begin. Paul spoke of "another law at war with the law of my mind." It is the age-old battle between the unconscious and the conscious, the objective and subjective, supraego and ego. Concepts do battle with symbols, phenomena with noumena, existence with essence.

Consciousness is the distinctive element of personhood. It is what makes us unique. Only we of all the animals are the object of our own scrutiny. This makes us breathless about ourselves, so breathless that we often neglect the unconscious. Indeed, we may even hide from it. Once they have achieved consciousness, remember, Adam and Eve hid from God (Gen. 3:8). In Paul's metaphor, the unconscious, if we may call it that, is at war with the conscious, the divine with the human, the "law of God," in his language, with the "law of sin" (Rom. 7:25).

We are so mesmerized by the achievements of the ego that we have to be forced by our dark dreams and dark emotions to see the treasures *of darkness, the achievements of the* supra*ego, what we are being fashioned* into *as well as what we are fashioning ourselves.*

The trouble is that consciousness feeds on itself. Its achievements are so vast that it is virtually impossible for it to keep itself in perspective. After all, when you are president of the company or the parent of three beautiful children, you have little time for your dreams and dark emotions. Consequently, the self is *constantly* unbalanced. That is why the unconscious has to keep asserting itself "darkly" (1 Cor. 13:12, *KJV*). And it is a fact that most dreams *are* dark. Most are negative, according to the scientific data. Consciousness conceals the unconscious. Therefore the unconscious has to reveal itself. And since we are not open to it naturally, the revelations have to be "unnatural," in terms of dreams and emotions that we would normally avoid. Concealing the unconscious is precisely the temptation Jesus resisted when He was alone in the wilderness, bewildered by the war within Him between the conscious and the unconscious, between ego and God. Note that they were all temptations of the ego, to indulge Himself or "make a name" for Himself.

Consciousness needs to become aware of the real personality, which is *both* conscious *and* unconscious. The irony is that such awareness comes through to us; we do not come through to it. It has to be, as it were, forced upon us. We are so mesmerized by the achievements of the ego that we have to be forced by our dark dreams and dark emotions to see the *treasures* of darkness, the achievements of the *supra*ego, what we are being fashioned *into* as well as what we are fashioning ourselves. The images that force themselves upon us are not creations of our will. They are creations of the unconscious, where we do not will anything, as in a dream, where we are asleep and beyond willing. The greatest challenge to present-day rationalists is to hypostatize the unconscious, to grant it reality, to agree that it exists, to take it with the utmost seriousness.

Psychologist Gerhard Adler believed, contrary to Schopenhauer and others, that it is *not* the will which produces answers to life's deepest questions. It is rather the pre-logical (not illogical), primitive (not ignorant) matrix known as the unconscious, welling up spontaneously in children and those less consciously developed, which produces such answers.[1] "You must turn and become like children," Jesus said. You must use your negative emotions to stimulate your imaginations to see arks and doves. Children are highly imaginative—often without the aid of negative emotions. Adults, however, need the nudge, push, shove of the negative.

It is this deeper or inmost self which has the power "to produce a *more* meaningful and valid answer than the conscious mind with its clearer but necessarily more restricted view."² If we will only be aware, that is, conscious, of how these symbols are "throwing" us "with" ourselves, *that* is how we will be "healed" of our symptoms. It is how we will become whole. It is how the war within will be a Holy War. All three words—"healed," "whole," "holy"—have the same root meaning "whole, uninjured, of good omen."

III

The emerging of the unconscious is the religious process, hence "holy." Religion, in the root meaning of the word, "binds us back" to the rest of who we are. In Hegelian terms, self is the synthesis between the thesis of the unconscious and the antithesis of the conscious. Becoming who we are is the objective, among other things, of religion. Abraham became himself as he left Haran for the Promised Land. Moses became who he was as he left his shepherding to lead the people out of Egypt. Jesus became Himself as He refused to let the allure of the achievements of the ego conceal the superachievements of the supraego.

Religion asks the questions *Why* and *Whither?* Why am I here? Where am I going? The answers can only come from the inmost self as it is in dialectic with the conscious self. All unconscious and no conscious leaves us children or primitives. All conscious and no unconscious leaves us ingenuous adults. Religion reminds us that both polarities need each other, that Paul's war is the only way to peace. *Eros* needs *Logos*. Mother needs Father. Eve needs Adam. Ego needs supraego. Self 1, in Jung's terms, needs Self 2. Consciousness needs the unconscious. Light needs dark. We need God.

Let us say that mother is *Eros*,[3] Eve, longing for
wholeness, mother church, medieval culture, the unconscious. Let us say that father is *Logos*, Adam, the principle
of rationality, father time, Renaissance culture, the conscious. And let us say that both mother and father exist in
us, both woman and man, feminine and masculine, and that
our religious duty is to achieve their synthesis, and in the
synthesis create, as Andre Gide once observed, "the most
imperishable of beings."

In other words, we are not to let the war within be
won by either the conscious *or* the unconscious. A cheap
win is the most tempting of all. We cannot be so unconscious that we are not conscious. That is psychosis. Nor
can we be so conscious that we are not unconscious. That
is egomania. Religion is the force within us keeping the
two in creative tension. But it is also a procreative tension
because something new is produced. Hence the biblical
metaphors of "new creation," "born again," and the apoth-
eosis of the child, an age-old symbol of the self.

Religion thus is not the sublimation of instincts which
cannot be otherwise realized, as Freud thought. It is not
the sublimation of the drive for power, as Alfred Adler
thought. Religion is rather the force moving the self to
itself, binding it back to the rest of what it is. It is the way
we answer the questions *Why?* and *Whither?* It is more
than logical and deeper than rational. It comes from our
depths, from our inmost self in creative conflict with our
conscious self.

This is why Newton, the scientist, could write books
of theology. It is why Chardin, the theologian, could write
books of science. They were whole men, true Renaissance men. And the image each had was of the Whole
Man, Jesus, the Christ Child, whose wholeness was so
great it has been called holy, and whose holiness is so

great that we say it heals us. It heals the split, at least momentarily, between inner and outer self. "He is our peace, who has . . . broken down the dividing wall of hostility" (Eph. 2:14). The symbol had done its work. A treasure from darkness had been revealed.

Notes
1. G. Adler, *Studies in Analytical Psychology* (New York: Putnam, 1966), p. 187.
2. Ibid., p. 188 (ital. add).
3. Ibid., p. 156, citing C. G. Jung: "The woman in the psychology of a man . . . represents the principle of Eros." Likewise the man in the psychology of a woman would be represented by the same principle. "Eros . . . was a mere abstraction to Hesiod," hence not personified as either male or female. R. Graves, *The Greek Myths* (New York: Braziller, 1957), p. 58. Eros was later personified as a male god. Hesiod's is the earliest known reference to Eros, around 800 B.C.

7

THE GIFT
OF DENIAL

John[1] was the best example of a workaholic I have ever known. He prided himself on his seventy-hour weeks. He never took a day off, and the only play time he ever allowed himself was Saturday night. He and his wife would go out for dinner, which must have eased his conscience a little. He would rarely get home in time for the family meal, and when he did arrive the children would often be in bed.

"It must be my Puritan genes," he would joke to me. Or I would anticipate him with, "You sure are keeping the Puritan work ethic alive." I suppose he had to prove something to himself, but it was wreaking havoc on his

*family. Could he have been running from something, some
deep, inner place where he knew he wasn't measuring up?
The only way he could be himself was to prove himself.
But it didn't make him happy. Eventually it would do him
in, I thought, but I never told him that. I admired his success too much. He was at the top in his company.*

* * *

It is easier to think about work than to think religiously,
but religious thinking is not unnatural. Religion, among
other things, is the way we become what we were meant
to be. By our very nature we can think religiously; so we
can often grope our way to religion even in the dark. As
we do so, we are bound back to the rest of who we are,
including the parts of ourselves we are in the dark about.

I

Religion began for Peter in the dark. He was fishing at
night. He was in the dark about what had happened to him.
His best friend had been killed, and he could not understand it. He was having a hard time thinking about it—so
hard that he went back to his daily work and did not think
about it. "I am going fishing," he said (John 21:3). It is
what we all do, at times. Work can be a cover to which we
flee because we can follow its routine even in the dark.
The workaholic is often running from something, hiding in
the dark.

The word "Easter" comes from *Austron*, the Ger-
manic goddess of the dawn. But we begin our religious

journey in the dark, not the dawn. The light of religious understanding has not dawned on us. It was in his pre-Easter darkness that Peter thought to deal with the murder of his friend by not dealing with it.

Peter had run out on his friend. He had rejected Him. He had denied that he even knew Him. He was a failure at friendship. And he had not faced up to it. He had simply gone back to work, business as usual, returning to what he knew, what he was comfortable with, what he was not in the dark about.

There is a side of us that is in the dark. Most of us would prefer to keep it that way. We rise in our jobs, rung by rung. But the dark part is never brought to light. We do not do the work in the night that will bring us to the dawn. And so, when we celebrate Easter, as Peter was about to in the story of Jesus' appearance in John, it is only a half-celebration. We rejoice in the light, but we have not known the dark.

Whom have we deserted? Whom have we run out on? Whom have we denied? A spouse? A child? A parent? A partner? A friend? Ourselves? The rest of who we are? Peter was in the dark about himself. How could he have denied Jesus? What was it that had made him do it? He could not explain it. He could not understand it. He could not think religiously about it. It was too much.

Ironically, even though he went back to what he knew best, he came up empty-handed. His work didn't work. "That night they caught nothing" (John 21:3). We go back to our jobs after some crisis in our lives, and we find that nothing seems to work. We go back to our families after a family upheaval, and we find that the family system doesn't seem to work any more. "It's all ashes," a man said. And it *is* ashes because we deny the side of ourselves we are in the dark about.

II

"Jesus revealed himself" (John 21:1). It is how the dawn breaks. The light comes in the dark. "Even the darkness is not dark to thee" (Ps. 139:12). Jesus comes to us across the water, while we are at work, doing what we know, and yet in the dark about ourselves.

He revealed Himself. "Epiphany" comes from "Phanes," the Greek god of light. So does "phenomenon." We are dealing with the phenomenology of religious experience. The first phenomenon is darkness. The second is dawn. And yet the light is not yet great enough so they can recognize Him. He is standing on the shore and they have no idea who He is.

"Tell it slant," Emily Dickinson said. The Bible is full of slants. That is why it is not read. There are hints, parables, mysteries. "By indirection find direction out," Shakespeare said. But when we can have it straight from the newspaper, why take it slant from the Bible? Again, we do not think religiously because it taxes us. It is more work than our everyday work. Why bother?

Peter and his friends have not the vaguest idea who it is on the shore. That is the way it is in the religious process. We do not have any idea who Jesus is at first. "I have said this to you in figures," He says (John 16:25). The dawn breaks before the day. But in the half-light of the dawn we do not recognize the one who can save us, the one who can reveal the side we are in the dark about. And that is all right because it is a necessary phase in the religious process, a phase which cannot be emphasized enough as a phenomenon in the epiphany of God.

"Cast the net on the right side of the boat," the

stranger says. "They were not able to haul it in, for the quantity of fish" (John 21:6). The dawn is breaking more. They recognize him. He has helped them. In the desperateness of Peter's plight, in the dark about who he is, with nothing working out even on his job, *that* is when Jesus comes. Call it foxhole Christianity. Call it cowardice. Call it what you will.

Peter recognizes Christ in the moment of being helped. There is not a single instance in the Gospels of the disciples' catching fish without Jesus' help.[2] "Apart from me," He says, "you can do nothing" (John 15:5). But we don't believe that until we have been in the dark about ourselves. Because if we are only enlightened by all the lustrous things we have done, then we do not need the dawning of religion in our lives, we do not need Jesus. Then we stand in our own light. Then we cast our own shadow. And it falls on everyone else in a massive case of projection, "throwing out" on others all the parts of ourselves we are in the dark about and do not want to see brought to light. Such projection is exactly how people related to Jesus. It is why they killed Him.

But Peter "sprang into the sea" (John 21:7). He acted instantly on what he saw, by the dawn's early light. He didn't wait around to second-guess it. He didn't rub his eyes. He didn't say, "I can't believe it." He acted. He trusted his first response to the one who had helped him.

Embrace the one who helps you. Trust your response. Be spontaneous as a child.

III

It is light now. From the dark to the dawn to the day. Jesus makes a charcoal fire. More light. It was over a charcoal fire that Peter had denied Jesus. The charcoal may remind him of that. His dark side has suddenly become illuminated. Easter is the first spring Sunday after the full moon. It is when the dark side of the moon becomes completely illuminated.

Three times Jesus asks Peter if he loves Him. He gives him three chances to undo his three denials. And three times Peter says that he does love Him. It is the Gospel of the Second Chance, sheer lunacy to non-religious thinking. No matter how much we cover our darkness, day can break. Easter can come. Jesus can reveal Himself—in the face, the voice of the other,

---

From dark to dawn to day. From denial to appearance to action. That is the religious process.

---

the one whom we have wronged. At first we do not recognize Him, but then we see how He has helped us become the man or woman we were meant to be. The other was crucified for our resurrection.

Embrace the one you have abused. Embrace the one within you have kept in the dark. That person, that shady side of your character, reveals Jesus for you. That is *how* Jesus comes out of everywhere into somewhere, out of nowhere into now, here.

Peter is "grieved" (John 21:17). It is a *religious* phenomenon. He is hurt. He is suffering. He is in pain. But this is the very thing that is bringing him light, enlightening him about who he is, filling the dark side of the moon. It is the pain of repentance. He is "dying" about what he has done. And that *is* the metaphor. His old self is dying and his new self is being born. He is being born again, at Easter, through the pain of self-knowledge given him by the other whom he had wronged.

Jesus gives Peter a job. Action is how the dawn breaks and the day comes. It is how we carry the daylight into the night. At the end of each Gospel, Jesus gives the disciples something to do. The resurrection has not occurred for us, Jesus has not returned to life, if we are not doing something for Him.

In each of the Gospels, Christians are challenged to carry the gospel. "Go . . . and make disciples of all nations" (Matt. 28:19). "Do you love me?" Peter is asked. "Tend my sheep" (John 21:16). He means "Care for the Christian Church. Be a fisher of people as well as a fisher of fish. Go out to everyone. That is how you will illumine the dark parts of your life." They hauled in 153 fish—a number which perhaps stood for all the known species of fish in the sea.[3] "Go into all the world and preach the gospel" (Mark 16:15). "Repentance and forgiveness of sins should be preached in his name to all nations" (Luke 24:47). Give what has been given you.

From dark to dawn to day. From denial to appearance to action. That is the religious process. That is how we are bound back to the rest of who we are. That is how Jesus, the Savior, the One who makes us whole, comes into our lives. He comes to us in the dark, bearing the treasure, restoring the lost parts of who we are.

Notes
1. All names used in this book are fictitious.
2. R. E. Brown, *The Gospel According to John* (New York: Doubleday, 1970), vol. 2, p. 1071.
3. W. Barclay, *The Gospel of John* (Philadelphia: Westminster, 1956), vol. 2, p. 329.

8

THE GIFT OF BEING OUT OF CONTROL

He was out of control in our men's group. Between his sobs he said, "We called them gooks! We killed them like dogs!" One man put his arm around him. Another held his arm. Everyone was quiet. Then we went up to him and reached out to him and prayed.

Vietnam had been out of his control. He didn't want to go, but he would do his duty. Someone had to do it. He went as a first lieutenant. He said if you didn't get it from the Viet Cong in front, you were just as likely to get it from your own men in back. He told us he went crazy one day with a machine gun, blasting away at everything in sight uncontrollably. His sergeant finally pulled him away.

"I'll never show my face around here again," he said after his outburst. But it was only a momentary embarrassment. Person after person went up to embrace him. Many called him later in the day. "I feel good," he said when I called. His being out of control had put him in touch with a wound so deep it had been festering for seventeen years. And in sharing it with those who had prayed for him before, and would continue to pray for him, he was healed, at least momentarily.

* * *

There are times when we are not in control of what happens to us. You cannot control your spouse's behavior. You cannot control your children's grades. Often you cannot control your own career.

I

Peter was in an uncontrollable situation. There was no exit. It was beyond him. Note the passives—arrested; imprisoned; chained. Peter had come to the limit of his resources. He had been thrown into prison and was to be killed the following week. At the moment he was chained to two guards. Two more stood at the door of his cell. Any help would have to come from beyond himself. The physical would have to be superseded by the metaphysical.

What imprisons you? What guilt, worry, anger, fear chains you? What failure arrests you in mid-career? What force beyond your control threatens to undo you?

Discovering our limits is one way God comes. "My power is made perfect in weakness," God says to a suffering Paul (2 Cor. 12:9), who was chained to an incurable illness. But it was how God revealed Himself to Paul. It was how Paul learned, "When I am weak, then I am strong" (12:10).

What are you chained to? It can be the presence of God in your life.

When the Greeks spoke of the body as the prison-house of the soul, they were saying that the body had to reach its limits before the soul could be released. As Jesus said, "This is my body, broken for you." It was the way soul mattered, moved out in love and became essential to life. The *Logos*, the Revealer, is the broken One, chained to His suffering. "I am . . . the truth" (John 14:6) means that Jesus embodied the way of brokenness, the way of the cross as the way God is revealed. "The truth is in Jesus" (Eph. 4:21). When we are driven to our knees by what breaks us, when our bent knees and bowed heads are evidence of our brokenness, that is when God can emerge at last from the shadows of our cells and bring us the treasures of darkness.

> I will go before you
>   and level the mountains,
> I will break in pieces the doors of bronze
>   and cut asunder the bars of iron,
> I will give you the treasures of darkness . . .
>   that you may know that it is I, the Lord . . .
>   who call you by name (Isa. 45:2,3).

Peter was freed.

II

He couldn't believe it. "He did not know" the Bible says, "that what was done by the angel was real" (Acts 12:9). "Real" was the word for "true." It meant not concealed, fully disclosed, genuine.[1] Divine reality is different from human: it discloses itself and is what we call revelation. Peter could not believe what had happened to him because it was beyond human accomplishment. When we are freed from our bondage we cannot believe it has happened because we have not freed ourselves.

Chained to guilt on your right and fear on your left, you are released by God to live in the now, without guilt binding you to your past and without fear binding you to the future.

The way of imprisonment can be the way to freedom. Chained to guilt on your right and fear on your left, you are released by God to live in the now, without guilt binding you to your past and without fear binding you to the future. How can this happen? By being supine before whatever it is that is imprisoning you. Peter was so supine he was asleep. He was so supine he had to be kicked by the angel to get his attention (Acts 12:7).

Our problem is that even in our extremity we refuse to be supine. It is a word we probably have never used in our lives. We want to control what we cannot control. Whatever the emotional incubus to which we are chained, whatever keeps us so well guarded we are held back from life, whatever locks us up and keeps us undisclosed to our family and friends—we'll control it to the end. Either we repress it, which is to deny it. Or we suppress it, which is to put it off. In either event, we refuse to let it express itself, as we have seen, in order that God can make an impression upon us.

Peter completely gave in to the situation in which he found himself. It was beyond his control and he let it do what it had to do in order that God could get through. The fact that he was asleep was evidence that he had given himself up to what was happening to him in order that God could happen.

My friend had tears in his eyes as he told about some of the problems in his life that had shackled him and defended him against the presence of God. His tears manifested God moving up from repression through suppression to expression. For the first time in his life he was allowing God to "move out." God was at last coming into view, disclosing, revealing, becoming real, bearing the treasures of darkness. How did it happen? My friend found himself in a prison from which there appeared to be no exit. Yes, he had been there before. But always before he had denied or put off. Now he was supine.

Moses, supine before God at the burning bush, after going through denial and trying to put God off. Paul, supine before God on the road to Damascus after tragic denial. Peter, supine before God after his denial of Jesus, so supine that he "went out and wept bitterly" (Luke 22:62). His tears were the beginning of his turnaround. In utter brokenness, chained to the guilt of his rejection of his friend, when his life has "petered out," he weeps. And now, at this new point in his turned-around life, he cannot believe what has happened to him. He has been freed.

Neither can we believe it when God happens to us. We

do not believe we can see God while we are supine. It cannot be revelation. It must be good luck or hard work. We did it. Anyone but God. We cannot believe the reality of God in our lives. Consequently, it may not be until we are supine before what imprisons us that the noumenal will ever become phenomenal, the metaphysical physical, the ideal real. How ironic that in the twentieth century we call whatever is of this world "real" and whatever is of God "unreal." Our first priority, it may be argued, is to realize God.

A beautiful human being was dying. As she lay there, she moved us all a little closer to God. She talked of her life. She talked of her death. She talked of her love. She talked of her music, for she had been an organist and choir director for forty years. One night as I was reading the twenty-seventh Psalm to her, she began to sing it. She taught us how to live and she taught us how to die. As she lay supine before the onslaught of her illness, God made an indelible impression on each of us through her. We were in touch, as we say, with reality.

III

Even though we cannot control God, nor believe it *is* God, neither can we resist God. Peter found himself propelled through the iron city gate back to the home of his friends, who had been praying. Neither he nor God, it seems, could resist their prayers. "Earnest prayer for him was made to God by the church" (Acts 12:5). When he reached the house, they were still praying (Acts 12:12).

It couldn't have been worse for Peter's friends, either. They were at the limits of *their* resources. Peter's imprisonment was out of *their* control. There was nothing *they* could do. So they, too, became supine. They bowed their heads and bent their knees as a symbol of their supineness and of their solidarity with Peter in his brokenness.

Amnesty International, the Nobel Peace Prize-winning organization, tells of people in prison in Argentina, tortured in Iraq, on a death list in El Salvador. Prisoners of the month are highlighted in Russia, Mali, Haiti. In one year alone, 3,000 people were either shot on the spot in political assassinations in Guatemala or seized and murdered later in what Amnesty International calls a "government program of political murder." Our job as Christians is to be supine in prayer for those who are imprisoned by right and left in gross violations of human rights, to importune God in our solidarity with them in their brokenness.

> The Spirit of the Lord is upon me [Jesus said],
> because he has anointed me to
>   preach good news to the poor.
> He has sent me to proclaim release
>   to the captives
> and recovering of sight to the blind,
> to set at liberty those who are oppressed,
> to proclaim the acceptable year of the Lord
> (Luke 4:18,19).

Luke says that "earnest prayer was made for [Peter] by the church" (Acts 12:5). "According to the earliest sources," writes an expert, "common prayer seems to have been the order of the day."[2] "A special power of intercession," he writes, "was promised to the praying community"[3]—as opposed to the Stoic community, whose Stoicism was the main religion of Jesus' day and who did not believe in intercession.[4] Seneca, who lived at the same time as Peter, wrote about the impossibility of getting anything through prayer. The only point of prayer was to express resolution in the face of destiny. There was no certainty of being heard. There were no prayers for healing. None for liberation. No petitions at all.

The Lord's Prayer contains *only* petitions. Abraham, Moses, Samuel, David were great intercessors. Paul practiced intercession constantly. The early church viewed it as an obligation. "I urge that . . . intercessions . . . be made for all," wrote an early Christian (1 Tim. 2:1). Jesus prays for others as the last act before *His* imprisonment, and at the end He dies with a prayer for those who have imprisoned Him. "I would rather have an army against me," Martin Luther said, "than 100 men and women praying."[5]

Our job as Christians is to pray for those who are arrested, imprisoned, chained, be they friends or family or those we do not know but who are part of the broken human family. "If two of you agree . . . about anything they ask," Jesus said, "it will be done for them by my Father in heaven" (Matt. 18:19). It is an arresting thought. It is up to those who are out of control to prove that prayer is irresistible and that the iron gates will open.

However, we are not likely to believe that prayer can effect such release until we have first seen it release God in us by attending to our own images of incarceration.

Notes
1. R. Bultmann in G. Kittel, *Theological Dictionary of the New Testament* (Grand Rapids, MI: Eerdmans, 1964), vol. 1, p. 238.
2. H. Greeven in G. Kittel, *op. cit.*, vol. 2, p. 805. See Acts 1:14; 2:42; 1 Cor. 14:13.
3. Idem.
4. Ibid., p. 782.
5. T. P. Ferris in *The Interpreter's Bible* (New York: Abingdon, 1954), vol. 9, p. 157.

THE TREASURES
OF INSECURITY

9
THE GIFT
OF ANXIETY

They have tried everything for Jim, and nothing seems to work. He has gone through all the tests. They have brought in experts. Now they have told him they can do nothing for him. He will just have to live with his illness. And eventually die.

His wife and son and I were together as he underwent one of the tests. He was two floors below, and we were anxious for him. It was one of those tests where you don't know which way it will go. He could have died on the table.

In his room the next day, I was stunned by his resilience. He joked with the nurse and with me. It wasn't bravado. It was the deep, inner resources of the human

spirit, which were being given him through his disease.
God was somehow coming to him through his anxiety. I
marveled before the power of it.

* * *

The word "anxiety" comes from the Latin for "strangle."
We feel choked up, as we say. Our breath constricts. We
may even feel the breath of life itself cut off. We may think
of suicide. We sigh. We cannot get our food down.

There is, of course, a great deal of life for which we are
legitimately concerned—the children's schooling, the
mortgage, our jobs, the future of the country, a sensible
concern for our marriage, a level-headed appraisal of
where we are in our lives.

I

Anxiety may be defined as excessive concern. Strangling
is an excessive act. Anxiety is concern which "feeds on
itself," says the American Heritage Dictionary. Anxiety
hits us at points where we are most vulnerable and least in
control, such as health and death. We may be anxious
about our children. They may be growing up or grown and
increasingly or totally out of our control. We become vulnerable to all sorts of anxieties. How are they going to
turn out? Why didn't I relate to them differently? Why
didn't I raise them to cope with life better? Or we may be
anxious because we haven't had children yet.

We are anxious about our parents. How are we going

to care for them in their old age? Should they go into a nursing home or come to our home? After all, they took care of us when we were young. Of if they have died we ask ourselves, "Why wasn't I closer to Mom when she was alive?" "Why didn't I ever work out that problem with Dad before he died?" "Why did we drift apart and never see each other any more? Never write?"

Each of us has our own list of anxieties, but most fall into one of two categories, anxiety either about the past or about the future. Anxiety about the past we will call guilt. Anxiety about the future we call worry. In each instance we are robbed of the present. It is strangled, choked off. "The cares of the world," Jesus said, " . . . choke the word" (Mark 4:19).

II

One way to deal with anxiety is to accept it as "one of those things" and go back to sleep. That is how we try to loosen the grip, as we say, that anxiety has on us. We take a common-sense, calm, rational approach and say, "Look, Johnny is going to be all right. It will work itself out."

But, of course, the rational approach does not always work. Indeed, if it is anxiety, it rarely works. It may work for concern, but rarely for worry. Curiously, the word "worry" also comes from the root for "strangle." We wake up breathing fast, with our hearts pounding.

When common sense does not help, we go for more help. We talk with someone. And as we talk we sigh, which is a sure sign of trying to loosen the knot, to "come up for air," as we say. We cry, perhaps. We get "choked up." All this "lets a lot out." We "get it out there where we can deal with it." Such measures are helpful—until four o'clock next morning. Because if it is anxiety it will be coming back. It will rob the present by forcing us into the past with guilt or into the future with worry.

So we turn to books. "Everybody came with books," someone said to me when describing a tragedy that had occurred in her life. "Each person brought the book which had helped him or her the most. And some *were* helpful to me. Then I found my own books." But then it was four in the morning again. The books did not work. Her present was still being robbed by her past.

So we try prayer. Prayer is helpful, make no mistake, just as reading and talking and reasoning are helpful. It may even be we are no longer concerned. But if it is anxiety, it is probable we are still guilty or worried. The proof is those times during the day—let alone the night—when the present loses out badly, not just prudentially, to the past and the future, when we do not like who we are, when we are anxious about what might happen to us.

So we try another way to handle our anxiety. Since the creative route has not worked, we try the destructive. We eat, sleep or work excessively. Or we lose ourselves in other people. We rack up volunteer hours. We pick up people by the side of the road. We are sensational on the job and in the home. We may even become known for how much we give ourselves to other people. But it is a curious mingling of plus and minus. We unwittingly say a lot when we say that we "lose ourselves in other people." We often do just that—lose ourselves. It is another form of running. Proof is that the anxiety is back. And proof that it is back is when we start to lose the present again in the future and the past. It is a simple litmus test which all of us can give ourselves. Am I living more in the future or the past than in the present? If so, then I am anxious.

III

"Do not be anxious," Jesus said (Matt. 6:31). He always used a command when He knew it would be impossible. Whenever we are at our most vulnerable, there He is with a command. "Love your enemies." It was impossible. "Turn the other cheek." It was impossible. "Be ye therefore perfect." It was impossible. "Do not be anxious." Impossible.

*A*nxiety is a gift. It is a gift of God, a charism, a grace, a charismatic offering to each of us, a chance—to live in the now, to have faith.

That, of course, was the point—the command *is* impossible. We try everything and nothing seems to work. That does not negate our trying. It only says that our trying gets us only so far. Indeed, it many cases it does the reverse of what it should. The more we struggle, the more we strangle. The guilt and worry get mixed, and the present is lost for longer and longer periods of time. Insidiously, the more we try to "pull ourselves up by our own bootstraps,"[1] as we say, the more we fail at overcoming anxiety.

This was what happened to Paul. He was the prototypical achiever. He had a graduate degree. He was a leader in his field. He was going all the way dealing with his pharisaical past and his troubled future. And he was getting nowhere. Although it looked as though he were making progress, he had not moved at all. And he knew it.

There is nothing any of us can finally do to be innocent. And there is nothing any of us can finally do to be brave. *The only thing we can do is realize we can do nothing.* "I am nothing," Paul said (2 Cor. 12:11). If anything is going to be done about our anxiety it will have to be done by something or someone other than ourselves because we cannot do it. We go through everything—common sense, talking, reading, praying, drinking, eating, sleeping, working, caring—to find we can do nothing.

Anxiety is a gift. It is a gift of God, a charism, a grace, a charismatic offering to each of us, a chance—to live in the now, to have faith. Faith is living in the now. Anxiety is creative because it is nudging, pushing, shoving us to live in the now. We seem farther from God in anxiety than ever, but we are closer. It is unbelievable. But it is happening.

You *are* forgiven. You *are* protected. Yes, you tried everything. But that was only to find you could do nothing. Your anxiety throws you onto God. You have nowhere else to go. Indeed you begin to feel—and there is certainly no common-sense explanation now—that it *was* God all along, that the anxiety is God's means of reaching you, of God's coming to you rather than your coming to God. You did not need God, but God needed you, and *this was the only way God could get to you.* In fact, God *is* what enables us to view anxiety as a gift bringing us grace. And our response, our faith, is living in the now. It is being forgiven for the past and being nonchalant about the future. It is accepting what is happening to us in our anxiety as *God* happening, our being united with the rest of who we are. When you find yourself living in the present that is God at work. God *is* who enables us to live in the present.

God is choosing us? God is equipping us? God *is* the

One who forgives the past and secures the future? "Three times I besought the Lord about this," Paul wrote (2 Cor. 12:8). It was a terrible anxiety about a possibly fatal illness. "My grace is sufficient for you," God says to Paul. That was all there was. It seems like nothing, but it was everything. It freed him. It lifted the noose from his neck. It freed him from the guilt he felt as a Pharisee who could not, try as he would, obey all the laws and do everything right. And it freed him from the worry he felt as a person who was in constant pain and might die.

"For freedom Christ has set us free," Paul exclaimed (Gal. 5:1). He was a new man. "If anyone is in Christ, he is a new creation" (2 Cor. 5:17). It was his way of saying "whole." He could handle anything now, past or future. "I have learned, in whatever state I am, to be content" (Phil. 4:11). "I can do all things in him who strengthens me" (Phil. 4:13). How do we know we are new? Because we have peace. We can live in the now. No, not every minute, not even every day, but enough to know grace is reaching us. "We have peace," Paul said (Rom. 5:1). He was incredulous. How could anyone with such guilt and worry have peace? But it was there. It was happening. Faith is our response to what happens. "We have peace." I forgive you. I protect you.

Note
1. See the author's *The Bootstrap Fallacy: What the Self-help Books Don't Tell You* (Cleveland: Collins, 1978).

10
THE GIFT
OF FEAR

He was afraid as he sat there with me, afraid that his wife would find out, yes, but I sensed that there was a deeper fear. As we talked, it turned out to be the fear that he would walk out on himself if he walked out on her.

The other woman was not the one who called forth the depths of his inner self. "Deep calls to deep," the psalmist had written (Ps. 42:7). In a different context, to be sure, but only at first blush. The context for both my friend and the psalmist is God.

God is coming to my friend through his fear. At least that is a thought worth pursuing. Indeed, he has been more active in church than ever before. To be sure, being active in church does not necessarily mean being in touch with God, but in his case it does appear to mean just that. I sense a new depth in him, a new quiet, and all because he didn't run from his fear but was brave enough to express it. That old shibboleth, "Where your fear is, there your God is," just may be coming alive in him.

*   *   *

Nobody knows much about Mary. The story says she was engaged to a man named Joseph. She lived in Nazareth. She may have been descended from David, possibly Aaron. That is about it. Nothing more—except that she had some other children later.

It is almost as if the storyteller did not want to distract us with unnecessary details. The only detail that is given is that she was "greatly troubled" (Luke 1:29), and the angel had to say to her, "Do not be afraid, Mary" (Luke 1:30). The only detail that he gives us is that she was afraid.

The angel who came to announce the presence of God in her life frightened her. The shepherds were afraid (Luke 2:9). Zechariah was afraid (Luke 1:13). Paul was afraid (Acts 18:9). They were afraid when Jesus stilled the storm (Mark 4:40), when He cured the demoniac (5:15) and the woman (5:33), when He was transfigured (9:6). What are you afraid of?

I

Is it any wonder that the ancient Greeks made fear a god? According to a fifth-century B.C. inscription, fear "is put just after Zeus and before all the other gods."[1] Why? Because that was the way the gods were revealed.

"Fear," explains a Greek scholar, "offers access to . . . religious self-understanding."[2] Going all the way back to Homer, who was writing about 900 B.C.—around the time the early Bible-writers were writing—was the way you knew you were in touch with the gods.[3] It was the way you knew they were in touch with you. Fear "binds us back" to the rest of who we are.

Luke's word "fear" came from the root for "flee."[4] What are you running from? Intimacy? Job? Marriage? Children? "I am more responsive to the needs of my dog," a man said to me, "than of my children. When the dog barks, I let it out of the basement. When my children cry, I do not go to their rooms." Are you afraid you are not a good father? A good husband? A good wife? A good employee? We know little about Mary initially except that she was afraid. Why did Luke choose *that* to tell us about her? Because he knew that God can come to us in our fears. Our fears are angels bringing us God. God is the One who comes to us when we are afraid. "Hail, O favored one, the Lord is with you!" (Luke 1:28). Your fear is a gift bringing you God.

Fear went all the way back. It was deep within Mary's tradition. It went to the roots of who she was. Adam and Eve fled. "I was afraid," Adam, explained (Gen. 3:10). Jacob was terrified by his dream of the ladder. But his fear was a gift bringing him God. "This is none other than the house of God," he exclaimed (28:17). Moses hid at the burning bush, just like Adam and Eve, because he was afraid to look at God (Exod. 3:6). In the fear *is* the self-disclosure of God, just as when we are most vulnerable to other people we are most revealing to them. In the fear *is* the revelation. Is it any wonder the Bible makes so much of the fear of God?

Virtually all the great revelation stories in the Bible are

frightening. In all the accounts of the transfiguration of Jesus the disciples are terrified (Mark 9:6; Matt. 17:6; Luke 9:34). The people of Israel are terrified at Sinai (Exod. 19:16). The Deuteronomic code specifically enjoins the fear of God as the way of God (Deut. 6:2). "All the traditions of the self-disclosure of God," writes biblical scholar Samuel Terrien, "suggest in one way or another the element of *mysterium tremendum*. There is a mystery in divine holiness that produces . . . a sense of terror."[5] Imagine the most sacred story of all, the birth of Jesus, beginning in an unknown woman who is terrified.

*N*obody talks about the fear of God anymore, and that is why we tend to miss the love.

God meets us at our weakest. At our lowest we begin the ascent to the highest. God "regarded the low estate of his handmaiden," Mary says later (Luke 1:48). "When we are weakest," I heard a man pray, "God is strongest." When we are most vulnerable, we are most available. When we are afraid, that is when we can see God. That can be our burning bush. That is when Gabriel, the messenger of God, can bring us the message, the gift, of God's grace.

"The fear of the Lord, is the beginning of knowledge" (Prov. 1:7). Why? How does that make any sense? Because not until I am afraid will I begin to know God. I don't *need* God until I am afraid. "Serve the Lord with fear," the psalmist said, "with trembling kiss his feet" (Ps. 2:11). Talk about paradox! How can you have God in fear? Ask the shepherds. Ask Mary. Ask anyone who has had the love of God break in to his or her life. It has often been when they were afraid.

This linking of the fear of God with the love of God is one of the paradoxes of the Bible. The trouble is that we want the love without the fear, and then we wonder why we rarely experience the love. Nobody talks about the fear of God anymore, and that is why we tend to miss the love. "The love of God," writes our expert, ". . . is never separated from the fear of God'. . . because absolute love means total surrender."[6] This is what you never hear about in humanistic psychology and the self-help books.

II

What does Mary do? Nothing. She could have been killed. To be engaged was tantamount to being married in the eyes of the law, and to bear a child before the actual marriage was punishable by stoning.[7] But Mary does not resist. Like Peter, she is supine. She does not run from the confrontation. She does not try to self-help her way out of it. She does not seek solace in "positive thinking" and "positive mental attitude" and "possibility thinking." She say, "I am the handmaid of the Lord; let it be to me according to your word" (Luke 1:38). Whatever the fearful thing was doing to her, she would let it do whatever it had to do. And this is what it would do. "The Holy Spirit will come upon you, and the power of the Most High will overshadow you" (Luke 1:35).

To overshadow meant to release the creative power of God. It meant divine generation, just as it means divine regeneration when we allow our fears to do what they have to do in us. Astonishingly, no positive use has ever been found of the word "shadow" in secular Greek.[8]

Except for its use here in the Bible, in the normal Greek of the day the word "shadow" was always negative, always something that obscured the true view, always the opposite of reality—unstable, fleeting, empty, vain, worthless. Indeed, even today the word "shadow" is used in Jung's psychology to denote our fearful side.

What the Bible is saying is that such a shadow is precisely this fearful side that can save us. It is a gift. "Is my gloom, after all/shade of His hand, outstretched caressingly?" Francis Thompson asked in "The Hound of Heaven." The Bible turns the ordinary concept of fear as a negative emotion from which we must be self-helped, into the extraordinary notion of fear as the means by which we reach God, the *summum bonum*, self-fulfillment, wholeness, peace of mind—by whatever other name, the Golden Fleece of humanistic psychology and the self-help books.

Our shadow, the Bible is saying, can lead us to our "overshadow." The Holy Spirit can come upon us in our fears, and the power of the Most High can overshadow our fears. Jesus can be "born," so to speak, and we can be "born again." Our shadow, *if* we will stick with it, as Mary did, can lead us to our overshadow, and we too can be called holy, whole, the son or daughter of God.

The early Christians took what was unreal, fleeting, negative, shadowy, and turned it into what was real, permanent, positive—the overshadow, the Holy Spirit, not the evil spirit, the power of the Most High. Luke, on behalf of all of them, was making a tremendous statement about who we are: When we are afraid, *that* is when God comes. When we experience our shadow, *that* is when our overshadow comes. When we go into the dark parts of our selves, *that* is when the revelation of God occurs.

The image of the shadow employed the same word

that was used for the cloud out of which the voice of God spoke at the Transfiguration. It was the cloud of God's presence that led the Israelites out of their most fearful place, when they were fleeing Egypt. The shadow is God's presence all along. It is the overshadow. "And a cloud overshadowed them" as Jesus' face was transformed (Mark 9:7). It transformed their fear into faith.

Transformation is what is happening to us as we become handmaidens to our fears, as we let them have their way with us. No fear will be able to overcome us. We are protected by the overshadow. "Hide me," says the psalmist, "in the shadow of thy wings" (Ps. 17:8). "Yea though I walk through the valley of the shadow . . . I will fear no evil" (23:4, *KJV*). Even the darkest side of life, death itself, shall have no dominion, in Dylan Thomas's phrase, because it is overshadowed by the presence of God.

The *daimon* in ancient Greece was analogous to the angel coming to Mary. The *daimon* was the god watching over your life. To the Stoics it was the divinely-related element in all of us.[9] To Epictetus it was the conscience.[10] It was your gift, your genius. It was the personal intermediary which made sense of the cosmos, the world of abstract forces.[11] It was the messenger between the gods and us, like the Hebrew angel.

We are obsessed by our demons. We grovel in irrational fear before them. But we are possessed by our *daimons*. They fill the space that is otherwise in danger of being consumed by our fear. The very thing that threatens to annihilate us is what transforms us.

There are only two basic emotions, it may be argued—love and fear. All other emotions are derivative. Fear is a demon if it is not viewed as a *daimon*. It obsesses us and makes us subrational. But if we can see God incarnating in our fear, if we can see Jesus in it, then what appeared to be demonic can become angelic.

Love is a *daimon*, Plato said.[12] It possesses us and makes us supra-rational. But is it any wonder that love in Plato's *Symposium* is mothered by poverty? We are bankrupt in our fear until we can see the possibility of God in it. The love can overcome the fear *if* we can view the fear as a gift bringing us God. When loves comes, as Paul says, then we know with full understanding (1 Cor. 13:12). The subrational fear is transformed into the supra-rational love. "Love your enemies," Jesus said, those whom you fear. Paul called such love a spiritual gift (1 Cor. 14:1). So did Plato. The wisdom which understands love, Plato said, is spiritual.[13] Love is "the mediator who spans the chasm [between us and the gods] . . . and therefore in him all is bound together."[14] Such ideas paved the way for Christ, the incarnation of love, in whom all is bound together. "For God so loved the world" that God gave Jesus (John 3:16). In Him love beats fear. We are transformed.

III

But how can we perform the transformation? I do not think we can, alone. That is where the church comes in. The church are the people who walk with us among our shadows and so accompany us to our overshadow. Remember, it was the church who were there for my friend in chapter 1. The church are the people who are with us as we go into our dark nights of the soul, as we deal with the shady sides of our characters, as we are frightened by our children and our marriages and our jobs. It is as hard to believe as it is in the case of Mary's gift of fear, but what we read about the first church is that they helped each other with their fears. I suppose I have read the passage in Acts 2 scores, if not hundreds, of times, but not until I was writing this did I reflect on the sentence, "And fear came upon every soul" (Acts 2:43). Later, in Acts 19: "Fear fell upon them all" (v. 17). "Work out your own salvation with fear," Paul wrote (Phil. 2:12). Your fear is a messenger bringing you God.

"Fighting without," Paul described himself, "and fear within" (2 Cor. 7:5). It takes a vulnerable person to confess that. He said it to his church. I am a fighter on the outside, but I am scared to death on the inside. When he admitted his fear, that is when God at last got going in his life, and his shadow, which had haunted him for so long, could at last give way to his overshadow.

Now he could move out in love. He could accept other people, because he was bound back to himself. He could give them the gift of being with them in their dark nights as the Christian community had been with him in his. "Conduct yourself with fear," Peter said to the church (1 Pet. 1:17). Why? Because "trembling and fear," writes an expert, "bring out the radical and total dependence of the believer on the saving work of *God*, and this in turn leads to acceptance of the neighbor and is thus the *only* achievement faith has to offer."[15]

But faith does not even have that. Faith begins in fear, but faith cannot even claim that for itself. "Work out your own salvation with fear and trembling; for *God* is at work in you" (Phil. 2:12,13). God *is* the One who is coming to you in your fear. If only you will be a handmaiden to it. If only you will let it have its way with you. If only you will accept the others who want to walk with you among your shadows. Then you too will hear the voice, "Hail, O favored one, the *Lord* is with you!" (Luke 1:28).

Notes

1. H. Balz in G. Kittel, *Theological Dictionary of the New Testament* (Grand Rapids, MI: Eerdmans, 1974), vol. 9, p. 191.
2. Ibid., p. 192.
3. Ibid., p. 194.
4. Ibid., p. 189.
5. S. Terrien in *The Interpreter's Dictionary of the Bible* (New York: Abingdon, 1962), vol. 2, p. 257.
6. Ibid., p. 258.
7. D. G. Miller in *The Layman's Bible Commentary* (Richmond: Knox, 1959), vol. 18, p. 29.
8. S. Schulz in G. Kittel, *op. cit.*, vol. 7, p. 389.
9. W. Foerster in G. Kittel, *op. cit.*, vol. 2, p. 3.
10. Idem.
11. Idem.
12. Plato, *Symposium*, 202e.
13. Idem.
14. Idem.
15. Balz, op. cit., p. 214, ital. add.

THE TREASURES OF TEMPTATION

11
THE GIFT OF TEMPTATION

She simply would not go to counseling. In spite of the fact that her marriage was falling apart, she refused to get help. She didn't need help; *he* did. It wasn't her fault; it was his. There was nothing wrong with her; there was plenty wrong with him. She was fine. Sure, she had some problems. Who doesn't? But she could handle them.

It is that tough, hard exterior that is so hard to get through, so hard for the Lord to penetrate. And it is such an act. I love her, but I am too close to be helpful. I tell her it is an act, a front, that if she would only go deeply into herself she would discover so much more. I have given her name after name of people who can help her, but she will not go.

Something is going to have to happen to her. Something is going to have to break her, break through that hard outer shell to reveal the treasure within—namely God. I fear for her because it may have to be a big and terrible thing that happens.

* * *

I

Jesus had His own Jabbok, as Jacob before Him. He had His own wrestling, as we all have. The *imitatio Christi* is, among other things, to struggle with our demons in order that the angel may be released. "And behold, angels came and ministered to him" (Matt. 4:11).

It all began in the classic self-help temptation of self-sufficiency. All Jesus' temptations, in one form or another, were temptations to go it on His own. He had just received enormous power in His baptismal "identity crisis," and the temptation was to use the power for His own ends. It is the danger implicit in any "peak" experience. It is heady stuff, like the tower of Babel. The temptation is to tower over others, to be one's own God, to say with the early Hebrews, "My power and the might of my hand have gotten me this wealth" (Deut. 8:17). Indeed, Jesus was on a high mountain. It is a symbol of inflation, of being on top. It is the fantasy we all have: I can do it. It is in my power. I am in control.

And that is a necessary fantasy, make no mistake, for much of life. It is important that we have ego strength. It is necessary to our development that we feel our power. It is essential to be as much in control as possible in order that we be ourselves.

But then what? The experience of Jesus suggests that when we are at our highest we are perhaps most vulnerable. When we are most in control we may be least. *"If* you are the Son of God" (Matt. 4:3), the devil says. Was Jesus having doubts about who He was? "Command these stones to become loaves of bread." It was the temptation to materialism, to find His security in what He could do, what He could make, what He could surround Himself with, rather than in the God surrounding Him who could do something with Him and make something of Him.

"If you are the Son of God," the devil says, "throw yourself down" from the pinnacle of the Temple (Matt.4:6). Prove to yourself that you are who you think you are. Test the truth of the revelation you have just received. Test God. Transcend your limits. As with Adam and Eve, you will be "like God" (Gen. 3:5), and God "will give his angels charge of you" (Matt. 4:6). The ego after its mountaintop experience has so filled a person's inner space that he or she is tempted to play God.

"All these I will give you," the devil says, "if you will fall down and worship me" (Matt. 4:9). It is the temptation of political power. If He could only be the Messiah, then He would not have to be the servant. If He could only command from His mountain, then He would not have to walk in the valley. It is a demonic inflation played out in all the Faustian myths of our lives, that, if we seek self-sufficient power above all, we have made our pact with the devil.

With the word "devil" coming from the roots for "throw" and "across," the devil is whatever throws itself across the path of our becoming who we are. You can still see the spot on the wall in the castle at Wartburg, Ger-

many, where Martin Luther threw his inkpot at the devil.[1]
The devil is whatever throws itself as a roadblock across
our lives to allure us onto the side roads of materialism,
egotism, and imperialism, all of which are simply examples
of our drive toward self-sufficiency, our temptation to be
something which, in reality, we are not.

II

We proceed from temptation to humiliation. It is one way
to proceed if we want to participate in the *imitatio Christi*,
and the extraordinary thing about the Christian way is that
it is a way which works—if, that is, we have the courage
to move from inflation to humiliation. I am coming more
and more to think that maybe the cardinal religious virtue
is courage. Not faith or hope or love, but courage. It takes
courage to discover God in one's humiliations. "Humiliation" comes from the root for "ground," "humus." A
humiliation is what brings us off the summit of achievement to the lowly ground of failure. In the Bible's word,
we have discovered, it is a fall.

Adam and Eve fell. The tower of Babel fell. Israel fell.
"Let any one who thinks that he stands," Paul said, "take
heed lest he fall" (1 Cor. 10:12). "Though you soar aloft
like the eagle,/" God warns, "though your nest is set
among the stars,/ thence I will bring you down" (Obad. 4).

The word for temptation in the Greek means "to know
by experience."[2] The only way we are ever going to be
who we are is by experiencing our limits, which come to
us in our falls, our humiliations, when we are grounded,
when we come off our "peak" experiences, when we are
plagued by self-doubt, when we realize that economic,
religious and political power do not work but plunge us into

terrifying experiences of lostness and aloneness and alienation which imply that we are distant from who we know
we are.

---

*The greatest temptation of all is the allure of
power—that if I am economically, religiously and politically powerful, self-sufficient,
then I am secure, then I can be who I am.*

Our word "experience" comes from the root for "learn
by trying." So we try everything, we want to experience
everything, we go through all the devilish roadblocks
thrown up to divert us from the true course of our lives.
And the greatest temptation of all is the allure of power—
that if I am economically, religiously and politically powerful, self-sufficient, then I am secure, then I can be who I
am.

Curiously, our word "experience" has the same root as
"fear." No matter how materially secure we may be, we
still worry about our health. No matter how healthy we
may be, we still worry about our paychecks. No matter
how confident we are in our children, we still worry about
their progress in school. No matter how secure we are
with our parents, we still worry about their approval. Our
fears are toppling us from the mountain. Yet, apparently,
there is no reason not to fill all our inner space with ego,
until we have experienced a fall from the top of the mountain. Our fall is how we become subordinate. It is a necessary experience, or at least a helpful one, if we would
experience God.

We do not choose humiliation. Remember: grace is
passive. It is chosen for us. It is done to us. We would *not*

choose it. Only Jesus would. "[He] did not count equality with God a thing to be grasped," Paul said, "but emptied himself, taking the form of a servant" (Phil. 2:6,7), the lowest, most fallen of human beings. We will not fall until we are felled, by coming up time after time with experiences of not being on top of the mountain but rather at the bottom of the heap, afraid.

III

It is such experiences of humiliation which stimulate imagination, and imagination, we have suggested, is how God comes. From temptation through humiliation to imagination, three steps in the religious process, the process of being "bound back" to our baptisms and our original union with God.

The sufferings our temptations bring are exactly what are needed to stimulate our imaginations to realize we are made in the "image of God" (Gen. 1:27). One would wish it did not have to be so, but apparently it does. Because *without our sufferings we would still be on top of the mountain*. It is our falls from the top of the mountain that stimulate our imaginations to see that the mountain is Golgotha. It is our humiliations that enable Jesus to come. That is why Paul could say, "God . . . will not let you be tempted beyond your strength" (1 Cor. 10:13).

God is coming to us through our humiliations—if only we will have the eyes to see and ears to hear, in other words, to imagine. "Though you soar aloft like the eagle . . . thence *I* will bring you down" (Obad. 4). God tested Abraham in the sacrifice of Isaac. God tested Israel with the Ten Commandments. They were at a mountain, they were afraid, and God was coming in their fear. "*God* has come to prove you," Moses said (Exod. 20:20). In the very passage that Jesus cites in His temptations, Moses is saying to the people of Israel: "You shall remember all the way which the Lord your God has led you these forty years in the wilderness, that he might *humble* you, *testing* you to know what was in your heart" (Deut. 8:2).

The word for test here is the Hebrew word for tempt.[3] Satan comes much later in the tradition.[4] Satan in the Garden of Eden is later. Satan in Job later. And even here, in the temptations of Christ, a far later instance of Satan, it is, remember, the *Spirit* that led Jesus into the wilderness to be tempted. As with Abraham, *God* was putting Jesus to the test. The *gift* in temptation is that it is bringing us *God*.

The greatest temptation of all is to deny that the humiliations that bring the suffering that stimulates the imagination to see God do, in fact, reveal God.

Notes
1. W. Barclay, *The Gospel of Matthew* (Philadelphia: Westminster, 1958), vol. 1, p. 58.
2. H. Seesemann in G. Kittel, *Theological Dictionary of the New Testament* (Grand Rapids, Mich.: Eerdmans, 1968), vol. 6, p. 23.
3. Ibid., p. 25.
4. Idem.

12

THE GIFT OF GUILT

Gene carried a load of guilt over his drinking. It had jeopardized his marriage and career. He had wasted a lot of good years. But then he had gotten hold of it. That is to say, God had gotten hold of him through it. He told me how he had knelt down in his doctor's office and asked God to help him. He never drank again.

Such instantaneous healing boggles the mind, but when I reflect on Gene's life, it seems as though his guilt created an ideal opportunity for grace. He had believed in God and the healing power of Christ while he was drinking. But he discovered that believing something and feeling it could be two very different things. To believe in forgiveness was one thing; to feel forgiven quite another.

When we got together, Gene had no hesitation in talking about what had happened to him. It was the image, he said, of what the future held for him if he continued his drinking and of what his life would continue to be like without God. Those two images turned him around, he told me. They were what drove him to his knees. The trip to the doctor's office for his annual physical fused the images and felled him to his knees. He was, he said, eternally grateful.

* * *

We are all guilty. We have all sinned. And the question is, how are we going to see our guilt as a gift?

I

One response is to say it is not our fault. We may quote the psalmist—"Behold, I was brought forth in iniquity, and in sin did my mother conceive me"(Ps. 51:5)—in an attempt to pass our sin off as inherited and therefore beyond our control. It is the classic escape from responsibility for sin (and one which the psalmist himself avoids).

Perhaps the most persistent way in which this option is lived out is to blame our parents for our problems. "I was brought up in a difficult home," we say. "My parents didn't love me. My mother had enough problems of her own, and my father was always away on business, so it was predictable I would turn out the way I did—namely, full of sin and ridden with guilt."

We would do well, however, to stick with the psalmist in avoiding this first response to sin. "There is no persuasive evidence," writes a professor of human development at Harvard, "to show that most unhappy adults were

---

A *first step in seeing guilt as a gift as opposed to a disease is to accept responsibility for our sin.*

---

unloved as children . . . . Of the millions of children who do not receive adequate amounts of early affection," he says, "only a small proportion develop pathology, and of the group with adult pathology, a large proportion may have been loved during early childhood."[1]

II

A more persuasive response to sin is to say it is our fault. "I know my transgressions," says the psalmist (51:3). A first step in seeing guilt as a gift as opposed to a disease is to accept responsibility for our sin. It is to refuse to blame human nature or mother or early schooling or boss or anyone else. A lot of time is spent in therapists' offices talking about our parents, when we should be talking about ourselves and to our parents. To be sure, our parents have made their contribution to who we are. But the point of the guilt is to free us from what we were so we can become who we are. Such freedom begins in an acceptance of responsibility for what we have done. "I know *my* transgressions." Not my mother's, not my father's, but mine, O Lord.

I also know my transgressions *as* transgressions. I see them for what they are. I don't write them off as foibles or mistakes. I know them as sin. And with this knowledge of sin a new dimension opens up. If I do something against myself or my neighbor, God is involved. "Against thee, thee only, have I sinned," writes the psalmist (51:4). The psalm has traditionally been ascribed to David, whose sin was having a man killed in order to take the man's wife. God is involved. As opposed to other psalmists who take out their guilt on their enemies and call for their bafflement, shame, and death, this psalmist not only accepts his own guilt but realizes it is a matter between him and God.

With the introduction of God, the problem of our guilt immediately assumes a radical new dimension. It is no longer possible to pass the guilt off onto others. It is no longer possible to pass it off as inconsequential. We are now in a position to see how guilt goes to the radical root of our nature (the word "radical" coming from the root for "root"). And when the guilt does that, the images come. When the guilt is accepted to the point where it goes to our roots, the images begin to appear. David's psalm, like most of the psalms, and indeed, most of the Bible, is loaded with images. That might not be of particular note if it were not for the fact that the images are the very agents that are bringing the healing and turning the guilt into a gift.

"Wash . . . cleanse . . . purge . . . fill . . . hide . . . create." They are proof that I am not alone with my sin but that God is in there with me in the form of the image of God in my imagination, which is working overtime under the stimulus of my sin and its subsequent guilt.

III

I know my sin as *my* sin and *as* sin. Consequently, I feel my sin to such an extent, so radically, that the images begin to come. That is how I know I have accepted responsibility for what I have done. If there are no images, if I can sleep perfectly well at night, if I am not troubled at the office or over the sink, then I have not yet accepted responsibility for my sin and there is going to be no viewing of guilt as gift. The word "accept" comes from the roots for "take to oneself." And if I do not take to myself the full responsibility for what I have done, then I will be more and more weighed down by my guilt as an incubus to the point where I may never see my guilt as a gift. The gift in guilt begins when the images begin. And the images begin when God gets involved. And God gets involved when I move from knowing intellectually I have sinned to feeling emotionally I have sinned.

Is it any wonder that when couples come back from a marriage enrichment weekend they can't stop talking about it? Why? Because they moved from knowing about marriage intellectually to feeling their own marriages emotionally. In that feeling guilt was involved. No, it was not the only thing involved, but it was one thing, and a big one. No one can be in a marriage and not sin against the other in the marriage. One of the things the weekend does is release people from guilt, or at least begin their release. And one of the reasons the images flow freely is that people are in touch with how they feel. And one of the reasons they are in touch with how they feel is that they have accepted responsibility for what is going on in their marriage. They have taken it to themselves rather than taken it out on the other. And in that process of radical acceptance God is involved. It is a religious experience. As a participant once said to me, "Last Saturday night I had an experience of the living God."

"Wash . . . cleanse . . . purge . . . fill . . . hide . . . create." That is *how* God works. "Snow . . . white . . . blood

. . . bones . . . tongue . . . hyssop . . . break." "The sacrifice acceptable to God is a broken spirit" (51:17). It is our brokenness resulting from our guilt that gets the images flowing, like the broken bits of glass in a kaleidoscope. The images don't start piling up until the psalmist gets off his head and onto his heart, off his talk about sin and transgression and iniquity and truth, all of which are intellectual words, and on to his talk about what he longs for from God. "Wash . . . cleanse . . . purge . . . fill . . . hide . . . create" are all addressed to God. The gift is that the psalmist's guilt is bringing him *God*. It is *God* who is coming to him in the release of his images. And his images are released because he has accepted the fact that he is broken. And he is broken because he has known sin, really known it, as his and as sin, known it so deeply that it has known him, and he has felt it, and has groaned under the weight of it.

*T*he *energy released in brokenness, as when an atom is broken, is so great that it cannot be contained.*

The last thing, then, that we would want to do under these circumstances is to avoid our feelings by running from them, writing them off as "erroneous," projecting them onto somebody else, railing at the other as an enemy, talking incessantly about mother or father or system or boss or school or blacks or whites or Democrats or Republicans. First I know it, then I feel it. I go with the images that are going with me. And the final image—when I finally get off my head and onto my heart, when I finally realize there is more to me than my ideas, namely my feelings—is the image of brokenness. It is *this* image that God finds "acceptable." The accepting process has made *me* acceptable. My guilt has brought my God.

IV

But the process of guilt is far from over. The energy released in brokenness, as when an atom is broken, is so great that it cannot be contained. The gift of guilt is that it moves us to action as well as reflection. I think. I feel. I act. It is all there in Psalm 51. It is never enough to sit around and be beguiled by our images. They are so powerful they move us to act. "Snow . . . white . . . blood . . . bones . . . tongues . . . hyssop . . . break" are all there for a reason, and the reason is that our radical acceptance leads us to radical action.

The motivation for the action is joy. "Restore to me the joy of thy salvation" (51:12). The joy comes in the brokenness. It is paradox, the language of imagination, of religion, of the dark night of the soul. You look up from your chair where you have just written your images down, and there are tears of joy on your face. You feel released. You feel forgiven. You feel God. The gift of your guilt is that it has brought you joy. You are so excited that you can't keep it to yourself. Your joy has to be spread so it can be enjoyed by others.

The forgiven one wants to teach. "I will teach transgressors thy ways," he says, and they "will return to thee" (51:13). The release he has found in his darkness is so valuable he cannot stop talking about it. The man who talked to me about marriage enrichment couldn't contain it. He had to share what he had found—what had found him. You know it's forgiveness when you find yourself talking about wherever it is your images have taken you. And the psalmist is saying that we don't really *know* release from guilt until we have *done* something about it—namely, acted upon our release.

It is not enough to feel good about yourself and what has happened to you. You have to share it. That is the point of evangelism. The thing that has happened to you is so enjoyable you cannot keep it to yourself. You are experiencing the gift of guilt when you realize that your images are impelling you to action. And the action, of course, is to share the good news of grace. It is to tell people that when you went with the images of your guilt *all the way*, grace was there. And it is to tell them that grace was *not* there *until* you had gone all the way with your images. The proof that it was not there was that you did not experience joy or find yourself out there talking about what had happened to you.

Indeed, it is at this point that the psalmist says he will not only teach but sing. "My tongue will sing aloud of thy deliverance . . . and my mouth shall show forth thy praise" (51:14,15). He will go back to his congregation and tell there, too, the good news of what has happened to him. That will encourage others to go with the flow of *their* images, experience the joy of *their* Lord, and then go out there and share *their* joy with others.

He rejoices with those who were with him through his time of trouble. He rejoices with those who had loved him enough to stand by him while he stood aside for his images. It was Nathan who got the flow of David's images going by helping him accept what he had done, really feel it and then act upon it. Is it any wonder, then, that Nathan's name, too, was put at the top of the psalm?

The church are the people who love us so much that

they will be with us in our guilt. They love us so much that they will urge us to go with the flow of our images. How would we ever know the grace without the guilt? "Snow ... white ... blood ... bones ... tongue ... hyssop ... break ... teach ... sing." Go with the flow of your images.

Note
1. J. Kagan, "The Parental Love Trap," *Psychology Today*, August, 1978.

13

THE GIFT
OF ANGER

He was furious with the other coach for "boarding" his kids. They were playing Little League soccer, and when you play it indoors you inevitably hit the walls. It's another thing, though, to *push* the other players into the walls, and when that begins to happen regularly it appears to be part of the other team's strategy. So he lit into the referee in front of both teams and the parents. "I blew my top," he said. He is still smarting from the unfairness of it.

But he is also remorseful. He is not proud of his behavior. "I lost it," he explains. He knew he was out of control, and now he realizes he presented a poor role model for his kids. "What can I do about it?" he asked a group of us. We gave him all sorts of well-meaning advice—from apologiz-

ing to the referee to apologizing to the kids and the other coach. He would certainly apologize to the kids at their next practice, but he was wondering if he shouldn't apologize to all the others, too, when they next met on the playing field.

* * *

The first thing Jesus did the day after He entered Jerusalem was drive the money-changers out of the Temple. It is astonishing that one man could have done what He did, but He did it. It is the best example in the New Testament of the righteousness of anger.

He was also angry at the Pharisees. "He looked around at them with anger, grieved at their hardness of heart" (Mark 3:5). "Woe to you, scribes and Pharisees, hypocrites! because you shut the kingdom of heaven against [people]" (Matt. 23:13).

They are both examples of the two kinds of legitimate anger in the Bible—first, when "it is a matter of directly championing the cause of God."[1] Hence it was legitimate for Moses to be angry at the Israelites for their apostasy at the mountain of God (Exod. 32:19). It was legitimate for Jesus to be angry at the religious establishment for standing in the way of God's healing of disease (Mark 3:5).

The other legitimate expression of anger in the Bible is anger at injustice.[2] The best place to find it is in the prophets. "I am full of the wrath of the Lord," says Jeremiah. "I am weary of holding it in" (Jer. 6:11), "Let justice roll down like waters," thunders Amos, "and righteousness like an everflowing stream" (Amos 5:24).

Aside from anger at apostasy and injustice, the Bible takes a dim view of anger. Although most of us tend to view anger as natural, the Bible, strange to say, does not agree. "Human anger," writes an expert, "is never clearly approved"[3] in the Old Testament, and, writes another, there are only two concessions to it in the New, both of which turn out to be warnings against it.[4]

Indeed, the Bible goes a step farther. "You have heard that it was said . . . , 'You shall not kill . . . .' But I say to you that everyone who is angry with his [or her] brother [or sister] shall be liable to judgment" (Matt. 5:21). Righteous anger is opposed to what God is opposed to, but, according to one scholar, "human anger is *never* described in this way in the New Testament."[5] "God's love," he says, "includes wrath, but love and anger are mutually exclusive in [people]."[6] Love "is not arrogant or rude . . . . It is not irritable or resentful" (1 Cor. 13:5). "The anger of (people) does not work the righteousness of God" (Jas. 1:20). Hence "the prophetic condemnation," as one expert puts it, "of human wrath in the Old Testament and New Testament."[7] Why? For the following reasons.

I

First, because it does not work. The Bible is pragmatic. It tells us not to be angry because anger accomplishes the opposite of what it is trying to accomplish. Anger begets anger. If you are angry at someone else it only stiffens the other person to be angry with you. "A [person] of wrath," writes the Proverbs writer, "stirs up strife, and a [person] given to anger causes much transgression" (29:22). Silence. Sarcasm. Tantrum. Violence. Spanking. Hitting. Abusing. Judging. Criticizing. Jealousy. They are all forms of anger and they do not work.

"See what it takes to set Mommy off?" writes Wayne

Dyer. "All you have to do is say this, or do that, and you can get control over her and send her into one of her fits. You may have to stay in your room for a short while, but look at what you get! Complete emotional domination over her for such a low price. Since we have so little power over her, let's do this some more and watch her go bananas over our behavior."[8]

Even more important from the Bible's point of view, our anger begets God's. "The nations raged," writes the Revelation writer, "but thy wrath came,/ and the time . . . for destroying the destroyers of the earth" (Rev. 11:18). "Wrath," says an angry Job, "brings the punishment of the sword,/ that you may know there is a judgment (19:29). "Cursed be their anger," Jacob says of his own sons (Gen. 49:7). "Everyone who is angry . . . ," Jesus said, "shall be liable to judgment" (Matt. 5:21). "The anger of [people] has sought to usurp the wrath of God and has for this reason become the object of that wrath."[9]

II

A second reason the Bible has trouble with anger is that it can be a cover-up for something with which we do not want to deal. Righteous indignation easily becomes self-righteous anger. As such it obscures the *gift* our anger is bringing us—namely, the gift of an undiscovered part of ourselves which can only be revealed by fear, but which we cover up with an outburst of anger in order to hide from our fear. I am afraid to face what my anger is obscuring because it would tell me something about myself I do not want to know. It is the fear of the unknown, the undiscovered, the darkness surrounding the treasure—in reality the fear of God in my life, that I cover up with my illegitimate—not my legitimate—anger.

Job, the Bible's angry man, kept avoiding the truth about himself. The person who thought he was righteous was actually self-righteous, and he took out his fear of self-discovery, of God-discovery, on his friends and on God. He shook his fist at God because he did not want to face the truth about himself—namely, that he had not found out all there was to find out about Job and that he was avoiding the process of self-discovery, a process that can lead to God.

> *The Bible is saying that the gift of the negative emotion is that it is bringing us God—*if *we will let it, if we will not run from it in self-help, and if we will not run from it by giving full vent to our anger.*

Anger out is almost always anger in. I take out on you what I do not like in me. Something in you makes me angry because I have not learned how to deal with it in me. Not always, of course, but often. And, the Bible says, most often. It is extremely rare that I find myself in what the Bible calls legitimate anger, anger about unfaithfulness to God or injustice to others.

The best test of anger is to ask ourselves whether we are in it for ourselves or for the poor in spirit and the poor in money. Are we in it for faith and justice, as Jesus was in Jerusalem, or are we in it for covering up something we do not want to deal with in ourselves? The Bible, being realistic, says that we rarely experience selfless anger, as Jesus did. It is almost always selfish.

Saul against Jonathan is an example of illegitimate anger (1 Sam. 20:30). Potiphar against Joseph (Gen.

39:19). Ahab against Elijah (1 Kings 20:43). Asa against
the seer (2 Chron. 16:10). Uzziah against the priests (2
Chron. 26:19). The Pharisees against Jesus (Mark 3:6).
The mobs against the Christians (Acts 19:28). Samuel
against God for the choice of Saul (1 Sam.15:11). David
against God for the death of his friend (2 Sam. 6:8). Job
against God for his fear of self-discovery (Job 9:14). Jonah
against God because of God's mercy to people Jonah hated
(Jonah 4:1). The elder son against his father in the story of
the prodigal son because of his jealousy of his brother
(Luke 15:28). We take out on God, as well as on our family
and friends, our fear of being led into a new dimension of
who we are.

III

So the Bible comes down hard on anger, in the third place,
because it stands in the way of God. We do not see our
anger as a cover-up for our fear, and we do not see our
fear as an angel bearing the gift of God. That is the point at
which many of us part company with Dr. Dyer and the self-
help books. Precisely the *wrong* way to deal with the negative emotion of anger is to try to self-help our way out of
it. The Bible is saying that the *gift* of the negative emotion
is that it is bringing us God—*if* we will let it, if we will not
run from it in self-help, and if we will not run from it by giving full vent to our anger.

In their anger, the people of Jesus' home town rejected
God and ran Jesus out of town. In their rage—it is the
word the New Testament uses—the mob at Ephesus
rioted against the Christians, rejecting the gift of God
(Acts 19:28). Pharaoh despised Moses, refusing the gift of
God (Heb. 11:27). Paul, "breathing threats and murder

against the disciples of the Lord" (Acts 9:1), refused again and again the gift of Christ. They were unable to see that their anger was a messenger from their fear, that their fear was a gift bringing them God, and that God *is* the One who can come to us in the basic negative emotion of fear.

Then suddenly it came to Paul that the very violence of his anger *was* what was bringing him God. "Saul, Saul, why do you persecute me?" (Acts 9:4). He no longer had to run from himself in anger when he could live with himself in fear—even the greatest fear of all, his own disease. Paul had come to the point where he could say, "Beloved, never avenge yourselves, but leave it to the wrath of God; for it is written, 'Vengeance is mine, I will repay, says the Lord'" (Rom. 12:19).

IV

Fourth, the Bible comes down hard on anger because it is, in the Bible's word, foolish. Not only does it prevent us from experiencing our fear and so experiencing God, it prevents us from living a balanced life and so experiencing God.

It is perhaps no accident that the strongest treatment of anger in the Bible is in the wisdom literature. Anger, say the Proverbs writers, is not a wise choice. It is, as Dyer calls it, "temporary insanity."[10] "A [person] of quick temper acts foolishly," says Proverbs (14:17). "He [or she] who has a hasty temper exalts folly" (14:29). "A fool gives full vent to his [or her] anger, but a wise [person] quietly holds it back" (29:11). "Be not quick to anger, for anger lodges in the bosom of fools," says Ecclesiastes (7:9).

Our word "anger" comes from the root for "painful." It

is the same as the root for "nail." We "nail the other to the wall" with our anger. It is painful for both. "There is no psychological or physiological reward for anger," says Dyer. "Yes, the expression of anger is indeed a healthier alternative than suppressing it. But there is an even healthier stance—not having the anger at all.[11]

Dyer may be closer to the Bible than he knows or wants to admit. "Refrain from anger," writes the psalmist. "Fret not yourself; it tends only to evil" (Ps. 37:8). "[Relax] and know that I am God" (Ps. 46:10). If this sounds as though the Bible advocates avoidance of anger, then it squares well with the findings of modern psychology, as Dyer implies. On the basis of extensive research, psychologist Carol Tavris reports:

> The psychological rationale for ventilating anger does not stand up under experimental scrutiny. The weight of the evidence indicates precisely the opposite: Expressing anger makes you angrier, solidifies an angry attitude, and establishes a hostile habit.[12]

The person you are angry with could well be the person you do not like to deal with in yourself. His or her face could well be an image of yours.

The Old Testament ideal was "the . . . [person] who does not err in anger"[13]—the person who is, as we say, "cool." It is also an Old Testament word: "[Those] who restrain [their] words [have] knowledge, and [those] who

[have] a cool spirit [are people] of understanding" (Prov. 17:27)—as opposed to what we call a hothead. They used that image too: "A hot-tempered [person] stirs up strife, but he [or she] who is slow to anger quiets contention" (15:18). "A [person] given to anger causes much transgression" (29:22). And most important, "A [person] of great wrath will pay the penalty" (19:19)—in his or her body, in intimacy, in knowledge of self and God. You have to be cool to realize that your anger is obscuring your fear, and that your fear is "binding you back" to the rest of who you are.

V

So what do we do about our anger when it is not in the service of justice or faith? We go slow, very, very slow. That will give us time to reflect before striking out. And in the reflection, if we are cool, we just may be able to view our anger as a gift, unwrapping fear, bringing self-discovery, revealing God. Maybe that is why the letter of James tells us: "Let every [one] be . . . slow to anger" (1:19). And why in Ephesians we read: "Do not let the sun go down on your anger" (4:26). Deal with it. Be cool. Pray. Talk it through with your spouse or friend. See the image it is bringing you of an undiscovered part of yourself. Act it in not out. The person you are angry with could well be the person you do not like to deal with in yourself. His or her face could well be an image of yours.

Notes
1. J. Fichtner in G. Kittel, *Theological Dictionary of the New Testament* (Grand Rapids, MI: Eerdmans, 1967), vol. 5, p. 394.
2. Idem.

3. E. Johnson in G. Botterweck and H. Ringgren, *Theological Dictionary of the Old Testament* (Grand Rapids, Mich.: Eerdmans, 1977), vol. 1, p. 356.
4. G. Stahlin in G. Kittel, op. cit., vol. 5, pp. 420, 421.
   "Only twice in the New Testament is human anger estimated positively" (419). In both places it is legitimate because (a) it is leveled against injustice (2 Cor. 7:11), and (b) it is inspired by God to "cause Israel to think" (Rom. 10:19)—i.e., against apostasy.
   The point of Ephesians 4:26, "Let not the sun go down on your anger," is to overcome anger quickly so as to "give no opportunity to the devil." The point of James 1:10, "Be . . . slow to anger," is that, in the next verse, it is rejected: "The anger of [people] does not work for the righteousness of God." Except for these two, which appear to view anger as natural but turn out to be warnings against it, and the two above, Stahlin indicates that "the judgment of the New Testament on human wrath is *always* negative" (italics added).
5. Ibid., p. 419, italics added.
6. Idem., italics added.
7. B. T. Dahlberg in *The Interpreter's Dictionary of the Bible* (New York: Abingdon, 1962), vol. 1, p. 136.
8. W. Dyer, *Your Erroneous Zones* (New York: Funk and Wagnall, 1976), p. 211-212.
9. B. T. Dahlberg, *Idem.*
10. W. Dyer, op. cit., p. 217.
11. Ibid., p. 210.
12. C. Tavris, "Anger Defused," *Psychology Today*, November, 1982.
13. E. Johnson, Idem.

THE TREASURES
OF MEANINGLESSNESS

14
THE GIFT OF ALIENATION

He has been looking for himself for years. And he has such gifts. He is one of the brightest and most personable people I know, but he just can't seem to "get it together." I have suggested a new job, a new way of looking at himself, a new way of relating to his wife and kids, but nothing seems to work. He isn't ready to change. It will take a miracle to get him to.

The miracle may come in strange form, like the burning bush for Moses. Perhaps his wife will leave him. Perhaps he will lose his job or be demoted. Perhaps his health will fail. Whatever it is, it will have to be something from the outside obtruding on his consciousness, or he will not change.

Maybe he shouldn't change. Maybe he is all right just

as he is. Maybe this is all he was meant to be and this is all God has in store for him. I'm not so sure. If he were satisfied, why would he be drinking so much? Why would he be recording his dreams and nightmares and writing long essays in a journal?

The fascinating thing is that he plays it out in the context of God. He is a strong church member, a participant in one of our small groups. He talks regularly with me or one of the other pastors, and is immensely creative in things religious, even to the point of considering seminary.

* * *

No doubt we would all like to have a burning bush experience. At the same time, most of us probably doubt that we ever will. The reason it happened to Moses, we say, was the peculiar constellation of circumstances surrounding him. While those circumstances may have been evident in 1300 B.C., they are clearly not evident 3,300 years later. At least they are not evident, we say, in my life.

That is why we tend to give the Bible such short shrift. It happened then, but it could not happen now. The heroes and heroines of the faith were what they were because God came to them in a unique way. The bush burned for Moses, but it could not burn for me.

I

"Moses fled" (Exod. 2:15). Many of us are running from something. It may not be evident at first, but if we will participate in only a modest degree of introspection we may well be astonished at the similarity of Moses' circumstances to ours. He had killed a man, and he was in flight from the police.

What most of us tend to do when we read the Bible is fasten on the miraculous and forget the mundane. That is why we get to the burning bush before we realize who Moses was in order that the bush might burn. And that, too, is why we tend to put the Bible down rather than pick it up. "Don't tell anyone," Jesus was constantly saying about His miracles. He knew people would fasten on the miracle rather than on the circumstances which made the miracle possible.

*T*he fact that we so often flee is what enables the Bible to leap those 3,300 years and bring the burning bush into our own backyards. We have our own flight patterns.

Clearly we may not have killed someone, but equally clearly we may be in flight. We may be running from what we know we should do. We may be escaping from the rightful demands someone has on our time. We may have destroyed someone at work and be avoiding every opportunity to make it up to that person.

Yes, when Moses killed the man he was killing an oppressor who was beating one of his own people. But that did not make it right. In a fit of passion—and compassion—he took the law into his own hands. "Who made you a . . . judge over us?" (Exod. 2:14), one of his own people asked the next day. His praiseworthy motive of justice led him into a less praiseworthy act of impetuosity. He acted without authority and committed murder. That is why he was in flight.

Remarkably, we see this flight pattern playing itself out time after time in the Bible, as it does time after time in ourselves. Jacob runs from Esau, whom he has wronged. Jonah runs from what he knows he has to do. Elijah runs from the authorities, as Moses. Paul runs from the lost part of himself and, in a remarkable parallel to Moses, kills people (Acts 22:4; 26:10).

The fact that we so often flee is what enables the Bible to leap those 3,300 years and bring the burning bush into our own backyards. We have our own flight patterns. For some it is alcohol, for others workahol. For others it is running from close relationships. For others it is running from a close relationship with oneself.

Even when we do not deliberately run, we discover that we often experience the most profound alienation, as though we were far from home, far from the person we intended to be, far from those who love us, far from loving ourselves. We leave home for the first time, to kindergarten or college. We leave the safety of junior for senior high. We leave the safety of one job and strike out for another. Some of us experience pain in a marriage. And in all these experiences we feel a sense of loss, of homelessness, of being far from where we want to be. Moses left all that he knew and ended up in a far country. And when his own son was born he named him Gershom, which meant "Far from home."[1]

Perhaps the most profound sense of alienation we experience is the lack of meaning. We wonder as we sit at our desks or work in our factories what it all adds up to. We wonder as we reach sixty-five what it all added up to, anyway. We wonder during our first year in college whether this really is the right place for me after all. And we wonder behind the vacuum cleaner whether this is what we were meant to do. We keep asking ourselves,

"Isn't there something more to life than what I am doing?" It is this longing for something more that reminds us of our alienation from who we are and what we were meant to be.

The problem is compounded for Moses when it is glossed over. His flight takes him to a faraway country, to be sure, but it also takes him to a wife, a child, a prestigious father-in-law, a good job with an excellent salary and the very best in pension and social security. "Here he is," writes a commentator, "under the benign sun, the very image of freedom, contentment, and peace, leading a no doubt impressive flock to pastures along the lower mountain slopes."[2]

Without alienation there can be no integration. The way to "get our act together," as we say, is to experience our act's falling apart.

The whole experience of alienation gets layered over by contentment in the affluent surroundings of his new home. Talk about being cynical about the presence of God. Talk about having zero expectation for a burning bush experience. Moses was in good shape. Everything was together. A good wife, a good home, a good job, a good community. Who needs God in a situation like that? Little did he know that God needed him.

II

Not only is alienation a fact in our lives, no matter how much it may be layered over by our contentments; it also appears to be a necessity, and in the necessity is the gift. The experience of alienation seems to be necessary to stimulate our imaginations to the point where we can see and hear God and be "bound back" to the rest of who we are, the self from which we are alienated. God comes to us in the most profound depths of alienation.

Why else does alienation appear in so many calls if it is not necessary to hearing the call in the first place? Jacob. Hannah. Jonah. Elijah. Paul. Moses. The journey into self even began in alienation when Abraham left his homeland to wander through all the uncertainty of alienation to his new homeland. "A wandering Aramean was my father," the Israelites were to write. "And he went down into Egypt and sojourned there" (Deut. 26:5) on his way to his new homeland, a better one, yes, but one that he was not to reach, as the old story puts it, without "terror" as well as "signs and wonders" (Deut. 26:8).

The terror of alienation appears to be essential, the ancient stories remind us, to the presence of God. Maybe this is what they meant by "the fear of God."[3] Without alienation there can be no integration. The way to "get our act together," as we say, is to experience our act's falling apart. Moses had to be purged of his impetuosity so that the leadership he was born with could be "born again." He had to be tempted by the fires of alienation if he were ever going to see the fire of the burning bush.

Alienation is the way we beat inflation. Inflation must be beaten if the personal economy is to thrive. Whenever the ego becomes inflated through an excess of contentment, God becomes deflated. The purpose of alienation is to teach us the difference between ourselves and God. When the ego is inflated the difference is obscured because the ego is our God. Moses is told to take off his shoes at the burning bush because he is standing on holy ground (Exod. 3:5). Later the people of Israel are told to keep their distance from God's holy mountain or they will be killed (Exod. 19:12). The Hebrew word for "holy" came from the root for "distance." The holy is in the alienation.

Alienation stimulates the imagination. That is its gift. The idea of God is the mind's most imaginative concept. "The idea of God is naturally engraved on the mind of man," Calvin wrote. That may be, but it takes negative emotion to remind us. It takes positive emotion, too, but as we have said, this book is about our negative emotions. At our most alienated we can be most in the presence of God. It is through such "negative" experiences as alienation that the psyche reveals itself, the unconscious becomes conscious, the latent God patent.

> And you shall remember all the way which the Lord your God has led you these forty years in the wilderness [these forty years of your alienation], that he might humble you [deflate you], testing you to know what was in your heart [your imagination] (Deut. 8:2).

As we look back on our experience of alienation we are amazed to hear the word "God" coming to our lips. Remember, this is when God's name was revealed to Israel for the first time. We say that God was in the experience all along. God led Moses through alienation in order to humble him and so bring him to integration, to meaning, to having it all add up to something and, indeed, having it add up to so much that nothing could ever subtract from it—not even his final experience of alienation when Moses did not make it to the Promised Land. Can we even imagine that the one to whom the burning bush experience was given did not make it to the Promised Land?

But it did not matter. The fire had done its work. The humbling experience of alienation had stoked the fires of his imagination. Even in the repeated back and forth between Moses and God as he led the people, his imagination was bringing forth God. "The people of Israel have not listened to me; how then shall Pharaoh?" (Exod. 6:11). "Why didst thou ever send me? For since I came to Pharaoh to speak in thy name, he has done evil to this people, and thou hast not delivered thy people at all" (Exod. 5:22,23). It was just the way it was at the burning bush—back and forth with God. Back and forth with the outsider inside. Back and forth between alienation and integration, between not wanting to do it and knowing it had to be done, between the self that was known and the self that was being revealed in the intense heat of negative thinking.

III

It is no accident that the story is of a burning bush. Fire is an age-old symbol of regeneration, of reaching a new place in one's development as a person.[4] To Heraclitus fire is the first principle of creation because in fire creation could be destroyed, but out of destruction could come a new creation.[5] It is the phoenix principle, the resurrection motif. Fire destroys, but it also creates. Trial by fire brings Jesus (1 Pet. 4:12,13).

It was fire at Pentecost, when the disciples were regenerated from a dispirited band over the death of their leader into an "incendiary fellowship"[6] "on fire" with the gospel. It was fire in the haloes of the saints—to symbolize their regeneration from ordinary people into extraordi-

nary Christians. It was fire that led Moses and the Israelites out of Egypt—to symbolize their regeneration from
slavery into nationhood. It was fire that Ezekiel saw in the
heavens, representing new life for the nation in exile
(Ezek. 1:27). It was fire at the burning bush, representing
the power of God to regenerate, and at Mount Sinai:
"Mount Sinai was wrapped in smoke, because the Lord
descended upon it in fire" (Exod. 19:18). It was the same
in the *Odyssey*, as Telemachus says to Ulysses: "Father,
my eyes behold a great marvel: the walls, with the rafters,
crossbeams, and the supports on which they rest, are all
aglow with a flaming fire. Surely there is some god here
who has come down from heaven" (19:39).

Fire is the symbol of a major psychological
breakthrough—so major it has always been called theological. It is *God* who comes to us in our exiles, far from
home, in the profoundest depths of alienation from who we
are, kindling our imaginations with new life. Indeed,
Moses' own name came from the root "to be born."[7] The
name for God which was revealed at the burning bush
meant "I cause to be what comes into existence."[8]

Fire means God. It is the phoenix rising from the ashes
of its own destruction. It is Christians around the world at
Easter waiting for the rebirth in fire of the sun and of God's
Son. It is the mediator between forms, destroying one but
creating another.

Fire means God, but its antecedent is the dry brush of
alienation. Then, when the alienation has done its work of
deflation, the spark comes and the bush burns, and the
one who has undergone his or her "trial by fire" praises
God for the gift of alienation.

Notes
1. C.A. Simpson in *The Interpreter's Bible* (New York: Abingdon, 1952), vol. 1, p. 866.
2. B.D. Napier in *The Layman's Bible Commentary* (Richmond: Knox, 1963), vol. 3, p. 26.
3. For a fuller discussion of the reality of fear and terror in becoming who we are, see chapter 10.
4. J.E. Cirlot, *A Dictionary of Symbols* (New York: Philosophical, 1962), p. 101.
5. F. Lang in G. Kittel, *Theological Dictionary of the New Testament* (Grand Rapids, MI: Eerdmans, 1968), vol. 6, p. 930.
6. Elton Trueblood's title.
7. R.F. Johnson in *The Interpreter's Dictionary of the Bible* (New York: Abingdon, 1962), vol. 3, p. 443.
8. B.E. Anderson in *The Interpreter's Dictionary of the Bible*, vol. 2, p. 410.

15

THE GIFT
OF DOUBT

Sue came to the church in an agony of doubt. That seems paradoxical, of course, that she would come to the church as a non-believer, but there she was. "If I could just find God in my life," she said, "then everything would fall into place." She is searching, like Diogenes with his lamp searching through Athens for an honest man, and she will not be content until she has found the God she is looking for.

    But I wonder if she will ever find what she seeks. Looking for God is important, but I wonder if God's looking for us is not more important. Until the seeker realizes she is the sought, she will never find what she seeks. It's all a matter of moving—being moved—from the activity of the searcher to the passivity of the sought. "I would not seek Thee," Pascal said, "hadst Thou not already found me."

It is this turning, this conversion, from looking for God to being looked for by God that transforms doubt into faith. And I don't know that it will ever occur without something outside of our control happening to us. While faith may involve choice, it seems to be a religious law that you cannot will your own faith. It has to be willed for you by God through the events of life—either sudden, dramatic ones, as Paul on the road to Damascus, or gradual, seemingly uneventful ones, as John Calvin's speaking of grace as coming "little by little." Fortunately—if we can use that word—Sue is experiencing just such a trauma in her life now with some family and health problems. She is right at the conversion point, the turning point.

* * *

Some of us on a belief scale of 1-10 are at 1, and the problem that needs to be solved or at least resolved is how to move from 1 to 10.

I

Let us say, however, that faith begins as a choice. We examine the various options from atheism to theism, and we choose to believe that there is a God and that God is most fully revealed in Jesus Christ. Such a choice seems to make the most sense for us. We make the choice in Sunday School and confirmation. We continue to make it through the rocky ground of high school and college. And then, as our family comes, we want our children to have the chance to make the same choice. So we bring them to church school and ourselves to church and continue the process of growth in the faith, hoping that we can steadily climb the belief scale from 1 to 2, 2 to 3, and so on.

At its simplest this was the faith of the disciples. They chose to go with Jesus. They did not fully understand what they were getting into. Their journey with Him had its ups and downs. On the belief scale of 1-10 they were at 3, possibly 4. At numerous points they were baffled. For instance, they had tried to put their faith into action by healing a boy with epilepsy, and their faith had not worked (Mark 9:14-29).

Such rational faith is what Job had. He examined the options, we can assume, chose his faith and discovered, in the midst of a crisis, that it was not enough. "Work out your own salvation," we have seen Paul say (Phil. 2:12). He did. The faith that Paul chose was carried out to the letter of the law. Being a man of action, he became one of the leading faithful, a Pharisee. The only trouble was that, like the disciples and Job before him, he was to discover, in *his* crisis, that his faith did not work.

We have to move beyond "accepting Christ" to being accepted by Christ, beyond playing the hero and making one more rational choice in our lives to playing the slave.

It is remarkable when you think about it that the people in the Bible who accepted Christ as Lord and Savior were the very people who gave up on Him in the end. One of His closest friends denied that he even knew Him. His other friends broke up the group and were on their way home. Indeed, as you go back through the Bible you find case after case of people who presumably believed in God but were having the most incredible difficulty having a faith that worked. The entire nation of Israel wanted to return to Egypt rather than go on to the Promised Land. The whole rational-choice approach to faith seems to have ended in disaster.

In our own lives, we would like to move from 1 to 10 on the faith scale because we find situation after situation where we, like the disciples and others in the Bible, hold a faith that doesn't work. It seems to desert us when we need it most. We need help on the job, help in the home, help with a tragic event that has occurred in our family. The faith we have rationally chosen does not seem to be up to it. There is more doubt than faith.

II

Consequently, we may well find ourselves moved beyond faith as a choice to faith as a gift. One way that happens, as for the father in the story of the boy with epilepsy, is to come up against something in our lives we cannot handle but is handling us. We have to move beyond "accepting Christ" to being accepted *by* Christ, beyond playing the hero and making one more rational choice in our lives to playing the slave, the word the early Christians used for themselves (Rom. 1:1, Phil. 1:1, *et pas.*), and find the events of our lives more than we can handle on our own. Slaves were unable to make choices on their own; they *were* chosen. They were unable to do anything of their own volition; they had to be *given* the power. In one sentence, the boy's father moves from hero to slave: "I

believe; help my unbelief!" (Mark. 9:24). Among other
things, it is one of the few sentences in the New Testament translated with an exclamation point.

One way we move from rational, active faith to imaginal, passive faith is to *be* moved by the events of our lives.
The father was in a crisis. His rational, active faith was not
enough. When Jesus saw that he had made the movement
from active to passive faith, from hero to slave, He gave
him the help he needed. Our crises[1] are invaluable for
becoming who we are. We may never move from 1 to 10
on the faith scale without them. It is next to impossible[2] to
get beyond 4 on the faith scale without crisis, without
some experience of serious negative thinking.

There were two ways of salvation for Paul, of getting
from 1 to 10, of becoming who he was. One was the law,
the other faith. He gave the law everything he had. This
was what distinguished the Pharisees. They were fine,
upstanding citizens, community leaders in every respect.
But what Paul discovered in his crisis of conscience on the
Damascus Road was that the rational, active approach of
keeping the 613 religious laws was not getting him to 10.
It got him to 4, perhaps, but it did not get him to salvation.
For that he had to be brought. In the word of the stricken
father, he had to have "help."

The difference between active and passive faith,
between 4 and 10, is the difference between believing in
Christ and believing "into" Christ. The force of the prepo-
sition in the original Greek is extraordinary. Nowhere was
this kind of belief found in the Greek culture.[3] "Belief into"
was not even used in the pre-Christian Greek translation
of the Old Testament.[4] It was a "linguistic phenomenon."[5]
The first Christians used it as a dramatic way of indicating
the kind of passive faith that would alone bring salvation.

When I believe "into" Christ, I have been moved by

my crisis into depending not on my heroic ego but on
Christ who moves into my ego. The reason the first Christians called themselves slaves was that they needed an
image to remind them of their subservience to Christ.
That is why it is imaginal, passive faith that works where
rational, active faith does not.

Our doubt proves that rational, active faith is not
enough. That is doubt's gift. "Work out your own salvation," Paul said. That is the rational, active part, and a necessary one, a first step. "For God is at work *in* you" (Phil.
2:13). That is the imaginal, passive part, and a *necessary*
one, the one that brings salvation through some event in
our lives over which we have zero control and which we
discover is totally beyond all measures of heroism.

* * *

One way faith is revealed as a gift is through prayer. "This
kind [of sickness]," Jesus explained to the disciples, "cannot be driven out by anything but prayer" (Mark 9:29).
The things that happen to us drive us to our knees, which
is the way we begin to *imagine* God rather than *choose*
God. We may even have the feeling that we are *being chosen* for this particular crisis. "Now is my soul troubled,"
Jesus says as He approaches death. "What shall I say?
'Father, save me from this hour?' No, for this purpose I
have come to this hour" (John 12:27).

It is speculated that what happened to the disciples in
this instance of their abortive attempt at healing is that
they remembered they had been sent out to preach, heal,
and drive out demons (see Mark 3:14,15) but they forgot
to pray. "Whatever you ask in prayer," Jesus said,
"believe that you receive it, and you will" (Mark 11:24).
He gave them an image to make it stick: "Truly, I say to

you, if you have faith as a grain of mustard seed, you will say to this mountain, 'Move hence to yonder place,' and it *will* move; and *nothing* will be impossible to you" (Matt. 17:20).

The only trouble is, many things apparently *are* impossible. We pray for healing, and healing does not come. We pray for help in our crisis, and help does not come. Our loss increases our doubt. But doubt is a gift because it shows us that the rational approach to faith does not work. Prayer does. And the reason prayer "works" is that, *regardless of outcome,* prayer is giving us the images that allow the hero to become the slave. Prayer enables us to live "into" Christ. "No one can come to me unless the Father who sent me draws him," Jesus said (John 6:44). "Christ Jesus has made me his own" (Phil. 3:12). "By grace you have *been* saved through faith; and this is *not* your own doing, it is the *gift* of God" (Eph. 2:8). These are the great statements of passive, imaginal faith which supersede the statements of active, rational faith. We move from accepting Jesus Christ as Lord and Savior to being accepted by Him—in our crisis, on our knees, regardless of outcome, slaves in bondage to Him. Christ Jesus has made us His own. "It is no longer I who live," Paul said, "but Christ who lives in me" (Gal. 2:20).

III

Faith is a choice, faith is a gift. Faith is also an act. It is rational, it is emotional. It is also volitional. Salvation engages the whole person—thinker, feeler, doer. The word "salvation," as we have seen, comes from the root for "whole." The images that come to us as we are driven to our knees in prayer move us to act. They are the *power* of negative thinking. The power of the emotional upheaval has been so great that we find ourselves "moving out" to other people. Faith becomes love.

The highest virtue of the slave was obedience. "A new *commandment* I give to you," Jesus said, "that you love one another" (John 13:34). Love means that I believe in you. I have faith in you. But it is even more than that. Love says, I believe *into* you. I believe *into* you so much that I will be with you as you move from hero to slave. I will be with you in the dark night of your soul. I will be with you as your crisis breaks up the image you have of yourself and allows Christ to live *into* you. And you will do the same for me.

What I will not do is take away from you the negative thoughts that deepen your faith. I cannot. If you are my child, I will not overprotect you. Protect you, yes, but not overprotect. The opposite of faith is not doubt. It is worry.[6] Worry says I do not believe in you. Worry says I lack faith in you. Worry says I do not think you have what it takes to move from hero to slave, to become a child of God.

And what that lack of faith in another usually means is that *I* do not feel *I* have what it takes to move from hero to slave *myself*. So rather than acting toward you out of love I am acting out of my own insecurity and coming to you in disbelief when I should be coming in faith. A new commandment I give you, that you give one another the freedom to fail. That you give one another the freedom to experience the critical events of life. That you love each other enough to allow each other to experience the catastrophic emotions that can move you over from hero to slave, activist to passivist, rationalist to imagist, doubter to believer, mountaineer climbing from 1 to 4 to Christian.

Doubtless Paul's experience of being loved in his crisis

by Ananias and later by others is why he put love ahead of faith. "Faith, hope, love abide, . . . but the greatest of these is love" (1 Cor. 13:13). He must have realized that the very Christians he was persecuting were the ones who, because of their love, were enabling *him* to break through to faith and then remain faithful. He watched the mob kill Stephen while he held their coats and while Stephen prayed, in his crisis, "Lord, do not hold this sin against them" (Acts 7:60).

Seeing that much love must have convinced Paul of eternal love. "If we have died with Christ," he said, "we believe that we shall also live with him" (Rom. 6:8). "He who raised the Lord Jesus will raise us also with Jesus" (2 Cor. 4:14). "I am sure"—that is the faith, but it came from the love, from their faith in *him*—"I am sure that neither death nor life . . . nor anything else in all creation, will be able to separate us from the love of God in Christ Jesus our Lord" (Rom. 8:38,39). At last he could imagine God.

Notes
1. Crises, coming from the Greek for "turning point," can, of course, be positive as well as negative, although we usually think of them as negative. As has been pointed out, however, this book is about negative crises.
2. "Next to impossible" because there can be no conditions for the acquisition of faith. You can't box the Holy Spirit. "The wind blows where it wills," Jesus said (John 3:8).
3. R. Bultmann in G. Kittel, *Theological Dictionary of the New Testament* (Grand Rapids, Mich.: Eerdmans, 1968), vol. 6, p. 203.
4. Idem.
5. Ibid., p. 210.
6. E.C. Blackman in *The Interpreter's Dictionary of the Bible* (New York: Abingdon, 1962), vol. 2, p. 229.

16

THE GIFT OF PURPOSELESSNESS

There was a knock on my office door. It was one of our teenagers. She was carrying flowers and was on her way to see the mother of her lockermate at school. That morning her lockermate had thrown herself in front of a commuter train.

Every year I discuss suicide with the youth group. If life has no purpose there's no reason to live it. At least that is one conclusion you could draw, as this girl obviously had. It seemed to me that my young friend was coming to church for reassurance that there was, indeed, purpose to life.

It makes you wonder what our kids have that that one didn't. Not that our kids are better. You can't say that. But

*maybe they have a glimmering of a purpose that she didn't
have. Our chief end is to glorify God and enjoy Him forever, reads one of the great statements from our church
heritage.*

*A sense of purpose, that her life was going some-
where, that she had something to look forward to, could
have saved this teenager. And what bigger purpose could
you have than glorifying God?*

* * *

"In the beginning God created" (Gen. 1:1). God had a purpose. We are created for a purpose. Everything that happens to us is for a purpose, even our negative emotions.
We are en route, going somewhere, ascending. Life has a
goal, according to the Bible.

I

Sin is rejection of purpose. The word "sin" comes from
the root for "be." Part of what it means to be is the rejection of purpose, our reason for being. There are times
when we say that life is going nowhere. It is purposeless.
It is the opposite of Genesis 1. "And God saw that it was
good" (Gen. 1:10). But life is bad. We cannot see where it
is going. It seems to be going nowhere. It seems to add up
to nothing. Rejection of purpose is so realistic it is in the
Bible. "Vanity of vanities, . . . all is vanity, and a striving
after wind" (Eccles. 1:2,14).

> What has been is what will be,
> and what has been done is what will be done;
> and there is nothing new under the sun (1:9).

The image is of the circle rather than the inclined plane.

Some interesting work has been done on circles.[1] Peaks in the abundance of the Canadian lynx occur on average every 9.6 years. The same is true of Atlantic salmon, American wheat, and New England heart disease. Plagues of mice occur every four years; lemmings every 3.86 years. There is the 9.2-year cycle in prices of common stocks, a cycle which could not arise by chance more than once in 5,000 times. There is also the 13.2-year cycle in the index of international battles that has repeated itself since before the death of Christ. There are even the biorhythmic cycles in our own lives that are so much in vogue.

The word "cycle" comes from the Greek for "circle." The only trouble with the image of the circle rather than the inclined plane is that it suggests life is going nowhere. "Life is just one damn thing after another," said the noted Kansas editor, William Allen White. I am reminded of another writer, H.L. Mencken. "On all known subjects," he observed, "ranging from aviation to xylophone-playing, I have fixed and invariable ideas. They have not changed since I was four or five years [old]."[2] No inclined plane needed there.

Sin is rejection of purpose. "Purpose" comes from the root "put forward." In the Greek of the New Testament it came from the roots for "turning point" and "promotion." Sin is rejection of promotion. It is rejection of the events in my life putting me forward. Sin is going backward. It is returning to the back ward where we have stored whatever it is that is preventing our going to the fore ward.[3] We usually think of the back ward as the place for prisoners and mental patients, but each of us has his or her own back ward in which we find ourselves prevented from going to the fore ward because of some complex which so complicates our lives that it holds us back. It is the back ward that we talk to God about in confession.

God finds us in our pathos place, where we are too complicated for our own good, where we cannot see that our creation was for "good."

It is an interesting cycle in which we find ourselves. Our lives appear to be increasingly complicated through one complex or another that keeps us living in the back ward for days, or in and out of the back ward each day, and we find ourselves refusing the promotions that will recapture a sense of purpose, of life that is en route, going somewhere, ascending.

II

God comes to us in our back wards where we are continually cycling back to purposelessness. That is where God finds us. God comes into the stable, the back ward where it is dirty and real. That is where Jesus is found. There is something immensely purposeful about that. God finds us in our pathos place, where we are too complicated for our own good, where we cannot see that our creation *was* for "good," where we are so caught in an inferiority complex or superiority complex or other restraint that we cannot see the way out, the way forward. That is where God can find us. If life were *already* purposeful, there would be no need for God.

It might be objected that all purpose makes for no process. But with God as the purpose the process is not lost. The process is found. "Love God," St. Augustine said, "and do as you please." It is a classic theorhythmic statement of purpose. Because when we put God first everything else begins to fall into place. It begins to be placed forward and up. Even the most complicated areas of our lives—such as business or family or illness or some terrible sin left for years in the back ward—begin to move forward. But often we *won't* put God first until life, as we say, "loses all purpose." Thus the *gift* of purposelessness is that it can give us God.

Such a gift is possible because God has *first* made a move to us. "We love, because he first loved us" (1 John 4:19). God has entered the back ward. That was the place where God found us. God rescued us. We are "the measure of all things," a breathless Protagoras said, caught in his hero complex. "O foolish Galatians!" Paul said. "Having begun with the Spirit, are you now ending with the flesh?" [i.e., with your *own* power?] (Gal. 3:1,3). We *can't* end with our own power. It is precisely when we end with our own power that life cycles down into purposelessness, or at least insufficient purpose to handle the classic complications of life.

Plato rhapsodized about the "perfect man" who could be made so through education.[4] But there is not a statement in the Bible that makes *us* the goal, that makes *us* the subject of promotion, that puts *us* in the driver's seat for making the exit from the back ward to the fore ward. It is precisely the legacy of the Enlightenment, which gave us good government but bad theology, that has hoodwinked us into thinking that we can solve all our problems, that we can uncomplicate our lives through our own efforts. Rather, the Bible says, it is just such egotism that will stick us in the back ward for good.

It is when God moved into the back ward that we began to move forward. It was in the midst of his agony in exile that his nation was no more, that the priestly writer of Genesis, from the remotest back ward of Babylon, wrote about purposeful creation—"And God saw that it was good." Creation was for a purpose, en route, going somewhere, ascending.

In all the complications of your life, you too are for a purpose. You are en route, going somewhere, ascending—because your life is attached to God. *God is* what solders your life to purpose.

Notes
1. E.R. Dewey, quoted in *The Smithsonian*, March, 1977.
2. H.L. Mencken, quoted in *The Smithsonian*, September, 1978.
3. J. Hillman, in the *Dallas Institute Newsletter*, February, 1982.
4. Plato, *Laws* II, 653a.

THE TREASURES OF ILLNESS

17

THE GIFT
OF CHANCE

Why did it happen? When your own daughter is badly burned in an accident 400 miles away, it makes you question, and think. Why did it happen to her? Why does it happen to anyone? It was her left hand and she is left-handed, but her hand appears to be healing well, all things considered, and she has been fitted with a special glove which she will wear for a year to encourage the healing process and help prevent scarring. Then, at the end of the year, she will have another operation.

I

When I first heard about her accident, it brought tears to my eyes. I sat down in a chair and the image came of her in the hospital in all that pain. I did not choose my emotion. My emotion chose me. I was helpless in the control of my emotion, and that was all right. In the burn unit when they put you into the water, you scream. And that is all right, too. They specifically tell you it is all right to let out whatever you have to let out.

Why is that a gift? For one thing, because I do not cry all that often. It is not "manly." I have a tendency, therefore, to be cut off from the side of my life available through tears. My daughter's accident put me back in touch with a distant part of myself.

For another thing, tears are the marks of the soul. When I cry, I am in touch with my soul. That is to say, my soul is in touch with me. Not that they need to be tears of sadness, of course. Only three floors below where my daughter was, a young mother cried on my shoulder tears of joy over the birth of her son. I am not saying that our soul comes to us only in the so-called negative experiences of life. There are plenty of tears at weddings as well as funerals. It's just that whenever we are touched by tears, we are in touch perhaps with the most "gifted" parts of who we are. "Jesus wept" (John 11:35).

II

I asked for help. I knew that I had to share this pain in my life, and I did, first with my wife, Jan, then with a church meeting that night. As I picked up a man to take him to the meeting with me, I found myself telling him what had happened. And when we arrived at the home where the meeting was, I found myself sharing the story again. Then, at my friend's suggestion, we all held hands and prayed for Heidi.

Why was this a gift? Because I do not ask for help that often. It is not "manly." I have a tendency to be cut off on occasion from the side of my life available through others. My daughter's accident put me in touch with another distant part of myself. And, as my hands were held by their hands, and the distance overcome, I realized again how much I need other people to be who I am. And I knew that the manly thing *is* to be in touch, just as the manly thing *is* to cry.

III

I found myself receiving. There were cards, letters, telephone calls, expressions of concern everywhere. Why was this a gift? Because I daresay most of us do not receive all that well. We tend to be embarrassed when somebody does something for us. We want to refuse the gift. This time I could not. My daughter's accident had put me in touch with another lost part of myself. Through her pain I was covering another mile on my journey toward wholeness. It began to sound almost like the Christian faith. "With his stripes," I remembered, "we are healed" (Isa. 53:5).

IV

I got in touch with my needs. "Do you need me to come?" I asked her on the phone. "I'm OK, Dad," she said. "I don't need you to come." Nevertheless I went because *I* needed to go. And that was a gift for me because I am often more in touch with other people's needs than my own. I was forced to identify what I needed and then act on it. I needed to be with her, and I went.

Those who came to Jesus came out of their need. "Those who are well," He said, "have no need of a physician" (Luke 5:31). The well people, the people whose lives had not yet been upset by chance, indeed, the Pharisees, those who were desperately trying to program chance out of their lives with their 613 rules for living, were just the ones who never came to Jesus. When I am honest about what I need, then I can come to Jesus. My daughter's accident had reminded me of a central truth of the Christian faith.

V

When I got there, it was, of course, pretty bad. Twice a day they would come for her and wheel her away to the whirlpool bath where they would cut her bandages off, and she would work her hand through the water, and then bring it up and with all her strength try to touch her little finger with her thumb. And sometimes the pain of it would be more than I could bear, and I would turn away and wander among the other whirlpool baths and inspect the mechanisms and examine the water and talk with the nurses. And then I would return to my nineteen-year-old daughter, and I would have given anything, anything, to be in her place, so as to be able to take the pain of it off her for a while.

Coming back on the plane, it hit me. That is what Jesus did. He took our place. What I had all along known as the doctrine of the atonement I now knew as the pain of my heart. "I wanted to be there instead of him," a church member said of her son when he was in such pain in the hospital. Now I knew what it meant to be atoned for.

Before it had been a theory in my head. Now it was a fact in my heart. "Surely he has borne our griefs and carried our sorrows" (Isa. 53:4). "O my son Absalom," David cried. "Would I had died instead of you, O Absalom, my son, my son!" (2 Sam. 18:33).

VI

Then another gift came to me. I was worried that she would lose the motion in her hand, that she would be scarred for life, that she would lose her first semester at college and possibly the second as well. Why was *this* a gift? Because worry would do no good. "We will take one day at a time," the doctor said, and when he told me that he gave me a prescription for *my* life, not just for hers. The gift of worry was that it was forcing me to live in the present. There was no other way *to* live.

When we view chance as gift we are prepared for God. Indeed, God is in what comes into my life through chance.

"Take . . . no thought for the morrow" (Matt. 6:34, *KJV*), Jesus said. "Anxiety," Reinhold Niebuhr wrote, "is the internal precondition of sin." Why? Because it proves we are not trusting God. God will heal the wounds of our lives. "Three times I besought the Lord about this," Paul said of his illness (2 Cor. 12:8). And back came the answer, "My grace is all you need" (2 Cor. 12:9, *TEV*). Worry gives grace.

"Grace" in English comes from the root for "praise." "I

will bless the Lord at all times," said the psalmist. "His praise shall continually be in my mouth" (Ps. 34:1). The trick is to praise God even in the accidents of life, *especially* in the accidents because God is coming to us in what we do *not* plan even *more* than in what we do. Grace is what happens to us. Faith is our response to what happens. Works are what then happen through us.

We have seen that the word for grace in the New Testament meant "gift."[1] The trick in these things is to find the gift in them. I am like Diogenes with his lamp as I walk around trying to find the gift in a bad accident. The word "accident" comes from the root for "fall." It is the same as the root for "chance." Whatever falls into your life, praise God for. It is like a leaf, falling to the ground to enrich the soil.

"Chance," said Pasteur, "favors the prepared mind." When we view chance as gift we are prepared for God. Indeed, God is in what comes into my life through chance. We talk about the fall of humanity. We should also talk about the fall of God. God is falling into my life all the time. The very fact that I am alive is chance. Or is it God? My mother and father meeting—who could have predicted that? I called my parents on my birthday and told them how delighted I was they had met.

Other events may be chance—or God. The way you met your spouse? The way you got your job? The way you have good health? The way you are forgiven? The way you got promoted because you happened to "choose" the right parents, who gave you the right IQ, remembering that intelligence is 75 percent heredity?[2] As you look back over your life, you get the impression that chance just might be plan.

Now I am not going to suggest to my daughter that God planned her accident. "It is not the will of [God],"

Jesus said, "that one of these little ones should perish" (Matt. 18:14). But God *did* allow it, setting up the laws of thermodynamics and gravity that would permit beef fondue oil to flame and fall. And God *is* in it.

When I was in my deepest despair over her pain, after dropping my friend off at his home when the church meeting was over, I turned on the radio and happened on a station where a man was talking about how he had shared with another man a particularly painful place in his life. And instead of getting the usual solicitude, such as "I really hurt for you," and "I'll pray for you," his friend said, "I'm excited for you."

"Excited?" the man on the radio asked. "Why?"

"Because you may be learning something you couldn't learn any other way."

In only four weeks I had learned six things which, possibly, I could not have learned any other way. And the biggest one of all, out of my anxiety for my daughter, is that chance just might be gift. The accident was something that fell into her life to do something for her and for me and for others that possibly could not have been done otherwise.

When we ask the question, "Why?" we are asking the religious question. It is the one word on Dag Hammarskjöld's grave. When we ask the question, "How?" we are asking the scientific question. Why did did it happen to her? and Why does it happen to anyone? are questions which go to the meaning of existence. They go beyond fortuity. As Nietzsche once observed, "Those who have a *why* to live can bear with almost any *how*."

We must have at least enough faith to posit the possibility of meaning even in events that appear to be meaningless. We must live *as if* there were meaning in the event—

the accident, the disease, the sudden death, the blizzard. Knowledge comes later—through the experience that our faith was, indeed, vindicated. As we look back, meaning *was there* all along even though we could not see it *at the time*. That is why theology is almost always in retrospect.

Retrospect provides the big meaning here. God is emerging from the accident. God did not will it. God did allow it. And God is in it. "I will bless the Lord at *all* times," the psalmist said, not just the obvious ones. In other words, events like these can bring us God. The gift of chance is that it gives us God.

Notes
1. H. Conzelmann in G. Kittel, *Theological Dictionary of the New Testament* (Grand Rapids, MI: Eerdmans, 1974), vol. 9, p. 375.
2. B. Berelson and G. Steiner, *Human Behavior: An Inventory of Scientific Findings* (New York: Harcourt, 1964), p. 217.

18
THE GIFT
OF ILLNESS

My friend has been in the hospital now for weeks. We pray for him regularly in church. We visit him, too. We carry the Word of God with us. We pray with him. He has the best doctors. The hospital is superb. And nothing seems to work. He is virtually no better than when he went in. It is immensely frustrating.

Another friend was in the hospital at least as long. We prayed for her and visited her and carried the Word of God to her. She, too, had the best doctors and was in another top hospital. Eventually she got better. She now goes about her life as if nothing had happened. It is immensely rewarding.

* * *

A mother told me how her pediatrician had done all that he could to treat her son's allergies. Nothing seemed to work, and the doctor was about to give up in despair when he put his hands on the boy in his office and prayed for him. The boy was healed and has not had an allergy since.

There are seventeen healings of Jesus in the Gospels. Nearly a third of the Gospel of Mark is devoted to the miracles of Jesus.

I

We do not fully understand what we are dealing with in the area of spiritual healing. "Christianity is not a formula for explaining everything," Albert Schweitzer once said. "The greatest knowledge is to know we are surrounded by mystery." It is a mystery that people are healed. It is also a mystery that people are not healed. We are not in an area where there are simple answers.

We are, however, in an area where healings by other than the usual methods do occur. We have evidence, such as that from my friend and from the Bible. Indeed, Christianity is founded on the greatest healing miracle of all, the resurrection.

There are no conditions for this kind of healing. God cannot be boxed. Such healings occur with faith and without, with prayer and without, with the laying on of hands and without. We must not create a legalism or an idol out of a method.

Spiritual healing is not an end in itself. The end is the spirit, not the healing. The healing is a means to an end, and the end is God in the person's life.[1] That is why we can speak of the *gift* of illness because, healed or not, illness can bring the person into a new relationship with God. With its vivid negative images, illness is one way we experience the rest of who we are. It is brought to our attention dramatically.

The healing miracles were not thought of as miracles, particularly by Jesus. They were thought of as the Good News in action. He called them "works," not "miracles." They were acts of power. But they were considered normal and ordinary rather than abnormal and extraordinary. That will require a whole new mindset for most of us, but, what with people walking on the moon, and Egypt and Israel signing a peace treaty, new mindsets are not impossible.

We need not feel guilty about asking for healing. We do not go to the doctor's office and justify being there. It is enough to say we are sick and want to be well. It is the same with God as it is with the doctor.

There is nothing in spiritual healing that is inimical to medical healing. The two go hand in hand. Indeed, there is currently a burgeoning of holistic health centers and healing teams in which doctors, nurses, ministers, families, and friends will cooperate in bringing all the resources of healing to bear. As a doctor once said to me, "There is no question that my patients with a strong religious faith have more going for them in the healing process than those without."

The gift of illness is that it gives us all, sick and well alike, a dramatic opportunity to recover what is ironically lacking in the emotional lives of many of us, namely direct spiritual experience in terms of a direct, personal relationship with Jesus Christ. It is impossible to participate in prayers for healing and not experience, to some degree at least, new life in Christ. What has been an intellectual experience becomes at last an emotional, possibly even a life-changing one.

We need to realize, though, that spiritual healing does not always work. People stay sick. People die. This does not, however, invalidate spiritual healing. Francis Mac-Nutt, a graduate of Harvard with a Ph.D. from Aquinas Institute, tells in his book, *Healing,* how he sees such healings "almost every day."[2] There is always hope. Even when the patient dies, a new spiritual dimension has been reached.

In a church I used to serve our whole church prayed for a woman who had been run into by a drunk driver as she drove her son home from a hockey banquet. We had a service for her. We set up a prayer vigil in the church. We prayed around the clock, people coming through all hours of the night and early morning to the sanctuary. And she died. But the whole church had a direct, personal relationship with Jesus Christ that was beautiful. As only one example, we named our mission fund drive after her and raised, in three-year-pledges, more money to give to healing the wounds of the world than we had raised in the prior three years for building our new sanctuary.

II

God heals. If God did not heal, then what kind of God would we have? "For God so loved the world" (John 3:16). Can you imagine a parent loving his or her child and not doing everything in his or her power to heal the child? It is inconceivable. Yet we view God as a loving parent, while not believing in the divine power to heal. If God loves us and will not help us, then God is irrelevant. Who wants that kind of God?

Healing means treating the whole person. The Bible never divides us. That is why a book on emotional ills includes a chapter on bodily ills. The ancient Hebraic conception of human nature was of body, mind and soul together, a unity. Jesus came to save persons, not bodies. What we are trying to do in healing is restore the person to his or her original wholeness. Is it any wonder, as

The gift of illness is that it can bring us wholeness. It is in hospital beds that hard-charging achievers will often see for the first time that there is more to life than hard-charging achievement.

observed earlier, that our word "heal" comes from the root for "whole"? That our word "holy" comes from the same root? That the Hebrew word "shalom," which meant "health," also meant "wholeness"?[3]

The gift of illness is that it can bring us wholeness. It is in hospital beds that hard-charging achievers will often see for the first time that there is more to life than hard-charging achievement. The broken body breaks the imagination open to receive images of wholeness. I know a man with leukemia who was "held together" by such an image for three years. The cancer clinic in Fort Worth, Texas, directed by Dr. O. Carl Simonton, is dedicated to the reception and retention of such images.

Because of the body-mind-soul link, healing was often accompanied in the Bible by the forgiveness of sin. Sin is whatever divides us, splits us from who we really are. When we forgive, wholeness can be restored and healing can take place. God's love has a hard time flowing into us

until our love is flowing into others. The two commandments were put together—love of God and love of neighbor. "I love God," it has been said, "only as much as I love
my worst enemy." "Whenever you stand praying," Jesus
said, "forgive, if you have anything against any one; so
that your Father also who is in heaven may forgive you"
(Mark 11:25).

People prayed for greater love for a man and his wife,
and a cyst on the wife's shoulder disappeared.[4] A man
prayed a forgiving prayer for his boss who had been giving
him a difficult time for years, and the man who prayed was
healed of post-operative pain.[5]

When we forgive we feel forgiven. When we feel forgiven we begin to heal. It is the power of God making us
whole. And it affects our bodies as well as our minds and
souls. Because we are of a piece, a unity. God is willing
our wholeness. That is why one biblical commentator can
say, "Healing in the deepest sense consists in the forgiveness of sins."[6] And why another can write, "Because sickness was a spiritual matter, healing could only properly be
expected to follow a revitalizing of the relationships
between the individual and God."[7]

Again it must be emphasized (1) that there are no conditions which can be placed upon the mysterious healing
process, and (2) that the healing process takes place in the
person who prays as well as the one prayed for, as in the
example of a whole church praying for an accident victim.

III

Jesus is the instrument of healing. Not the only instrument
to be sure, but one instrument, and a powerful one indeed.

Imagining Jesus is one way wholeness can come. He is the ideal image of wholeness. "The power of the Lord was with him to heal," writes Luke, the doctor (Luke 5:17). Indeed, Jesus was called the Great Physician. "Hardly another image impressed itself so deeply on early Christian tradition as that of Jesus as the Great Physician."[8]

The Good News was that Jesus "saves." It meant "to make whole," or "cure."[9] "Your faith has saved you," He said to the woman who touched His garment (Mark 5:34). "Your faith has saved you," He said to the blind beggar (Mark 10:52). "Your faith has saved you," He said to the leper (Luke 17:19). "Save" was the New Testament word for "heal." "In the healings of Jesus, the Greek word for 'save' never refers to a single member of the body but always to the whole [person]."[10] Jesus' name meant "God is salvation."

Another way to look at it is to say that Jesus has come to set us free. "For freedom Christ has set us free" (Gal. 5:1). He has freed us to be who we are, the whole persons God intended us to be. And the way He does that is to free us not only from "dis-ease" of mind and soul but from disease of body as well. Indeed, it was Christ's ability to free people from bodily ills that demonstrated His power over emotional ills as well.

"The kingdom of God," said Paul, "does not consist in talk but in power" (1 Cor. 4:20). Healing was an act of power. The lame, the maimed, the blind, the dumb were healed. His first sermon was about healing. When John the Baptist wanted to know whether he was indeed the Christ, Jesus said, "Tell [him] the blind [see], . . . the lame walk, lepers are cleansed, . . . the deaf hear, the dead are raised up" (Luke 7:22). He was not just *teaching* about the power for wholeness, he was demonstrating it. "Every time you meet Jesus in the gospels," MacNutt has said, "he is either actually healing someone, or has just come from healing someone, or is on his way to do it."[11]

The first church healed as well. The acts of power, remarkable as it may seem, were not limited to Jesus. They were continued by the early church, and they are continued by the current church. "Greater works than these will [you] do," Jesus said (John 14:12). Jesus gave them the same power of wholeness to heal body, mind, soul. He sent out the disciples with the power to heal (Luke 10:1). And they came back, writes the doctor, nonplussed (Luke 10:17).

We say, "Oh, but they were exceptional." Were they? "Is any among you sick?" wrote an astonished James. "Let him call for the elders of the church" (Jas. 5:14). Often now when we call for the elders of the church it is to discuss what color to paint the nursery. Churches should also have elders' meetings around the bedsides of people who are sick. "And let them pray over him, anointing . . . with oil in the name of the Lord; and the prayer of faith will save the sick man, and the Lord will raise him up; and if he has committed sins, he will be forgiven. Therefore, confess your sins to one another, and pray for one another, that you may be healed" (5:14-16). Made whole. Saved.

Notes

1. "This messianic and eschatological context gives to the earliest records . . . the distinctive impetus for which there are not the slightest parallels in Aesculapius or Dionysius." A. Oepke in G. Kittel, *Theological Dictionary of the New Testament* (Grand Rapids, Mich.: Eerdmans, 1965), vol. 3, p. 213.
2. F. MacNutt, *Healing* (New York: Bantam, 1977), p. 119.
3. R.K. Harrison in *The Interpreter's Dictionary of the Bible* (New York: Abingdon, 1962), vol. 2, p. 541.
4. F. MacNutt, op. cit., p. 139.
5. Ibid., p. 155.
6. A. Oepke, op. cit., p. 214.
7. R.K. Harrison, op. cit., p. 546.
8. A. Oepke, op. cit., p. 204.

9. R. Young, *Analytical Concordance to the Bible* (New York: Funk and Wagnall, n.d.), pp. 1043, 461.
10. W. Foerster in A. Oepke, op. cit., vol. 7, p. 990.
11. MacNutt, op. cit., p. 67.

19
THE GIFT
OF DEATH

It was a dying that took us all with it. Occasionally that will happen in a church. He was so central to our life together. Everyone loved him. He had such a fine mind and, unlike so many men in our culture, he was not afraid to cry. He was in one of our groups, came every week to the Bible study before church, stayed every week for the education hour.

When it was apparent that death was close, we all went to be with him in the hospital. There must have been twenty of us around his bed, all from his group, his "church within the church," as Augustine called such groups of Bible study, prayer and sharing. We shared communion with him. Everyone knew it would be his last.

*Then he explained, ever the rationalist, what they were
doing to him, how the disease was progressing, and what
the future held.*

*It was a magnificent display of courage. I was
reminded of nothing so much as Faulkner's Nobel Prize
acceptance speech. "I decline to accept the end of man.
He will not only endure, he will prevail." Here was a man
prevailing, and we walked away in silence before the
immensity of it.*

*But we also walked away in silence because we had
been in the presence of God. God had been in that circle of
love and leave-taking. The gift of our friend's dying had
been that it was giving us God. It was also, we hoped, giving him God because he needed God so much on his journey.*

*Impulsively I leaned forward as I left and embraced
him. His eyes were filled as I turned at the door and
waved. God was with him, all right. The gift of his dying, if
you could call it that, was that it was bringing him God.*

* * *

We were praying at the church for someone else in the
hospital in serious condition, and as we looked up after the
prayer one of us said, "I guess I'm a skeptic." With those
words, he linked himself with *Koheleth* or "the Preacher,"
a man who lived 250 years before Jesus and who wrote
Ecclesiastes, a work described by one authority as "the
most difficult book of the Bible,"[1] and by another as "the
most heretical book of the third century B.C."[2]

What Koheleth did is what most of us do. He cast an
observing eye over all that he saw, tested it against his
own experience, used the empirical method to arrive at

truth, and discovered what many of us have discovered, namely, that truth is problematic at best and nonexistent at worst. "What is truth?" Pilate asked Jesus (John 18:38).

I

The first thing an empiricist does is examine the evidence. "I applied my mind," writes the Preacher, "to seek and to search out by wisdom all that is done under heaven" (Eccles. 1:13). "I turned my mind to know and to search out and to seek wisdom and the sum of things" (7:25). "All this I observed while applying my mind to all that is done under the sun" (8:9).

And what he saw was not heartening. "I saw that under the sun the race is not to the swift, nor the battle to the strong, nor bread to the wise, nor riches to the intelligent, nor favor to the [people] of skill" (9:11). You cannot find truth in nature (1:9). You cannot find it in wisdom (2:14). You cannot find it in action (2:11). You cannot find it in history (2:16). The empiricist becomes the skeptic as truth eludes him. And, of course, we are hard pressed ourselves to find the truth in nuclear arms, a sudden death, the beginning of a disease, the loss of a contract at work.

Koheleth says that if we will be "realistic" (the trademark of the empiricist) we will soon see that it all balances out and that we cannot "realistically," give the edge to truth over falsehood, meaning over meaninglessness, good over bad. For every joy in our lives there is a sorrow. For every hope a despair. For every faith a doubt. For every love a hate. For every step forward a step back. For every progress a regress; every peace a war; every life a death.

It all balances out. We never move ahead. We are always stopped at "go." The line becomes a circle, and we are back at the cyclical view of history. There is "a time to plant, and a time to pluck up what is planted; a time to kill, and a time to heal; a time to break down, and a time to build up" (3:2,3). We are bound to the wheel of fate. Just as spring will come, so will another winter. Just as I am happy, in the next moment I am sad. Just as I believe in God, I also, if I am honest, doubt the existence of God. Just as I get over my cold, I come down with the flu. Just as I shout, I cry. Just as I cry, I shout. There is no moving ahead.

It is therefore of the utmost concern to Koheleth that we not pretend to meaning when there is none. He comes down hard on the so-called wisdom writers such as those who wrote Proverbs, who appeared to be smug in their knowledge of the answer to the riddle of life. The evidence, Koheleth insists, is that such optimism is not warranted. Just when you think you have the plan for your life figured out there will be another surprise, and you will be helpless before the apparent meaninglessness of it. "Time and chance happen to them all" (9:11). It is the opposite of seeing God in chance.

If you will be honest, the empiricist continues, you will observe that there is no absolute truth. There is no absolute security (7:1-12). There is no absolute morality (7:15-22). There is no absolute justice (3:16-4:3). Indeed, there is massive evidence to the contrary. The courts are corrupted (3:16). The powerful abusive (4:1-3). The laborers avaricious (4:8). The bureaucracy crass (5:8). The wealthy unhappy (5:10; 6:2). The good oppressed (4:1-3). The evil successful (7:15).

Consequently, the empiricist has what the man looking up from prayer had: a healthy skepticism. "Man cannot find out the work that is done under the sun. However much man may toil in seeking, he will not find it out; even though a wise man claims to know, he cannot find it out" (8:17). All of which is a healthy recognition of the limits of reason. It is a reality check against the cardinal sin of the empiricist, which is arrogance.

We all know bright people who think they know everything. We also know bright people who claim they know nothing. And it is to this second extreme that the bright Koheleth tends. Just as the cardinal sin of the empiricist is arrogance, so the number-one danger for the empiricist is paralysis. Because I do not know, I cannot act. Paralysis was Hamlet's problem. "Thinking too precisely on th'event," Shakespeare wrote, "he failed to act." And Koheleth comes perilously close to paralysis even as he berates his fellow empiricists for arrogance. Thinking, he says, "is an unhappy business . . . to be busy with" (1:13). And the temptation is to give up, to get your college degree or promotion and never be busy again with religious questions.

The last piece of evidence the empiricist observes is the most damaging. It is death. Death is the great absurdity. The fate of people and the fate of beasts is the same, he observes. As one dies, so dies the other. They share the same breath, and we have no advantage over the beasts. "All go to one place; all are from the dust, and all turn to dust again" (3:19,20). Death makes everything relative. Even wisdom, reason, education, what separates us from the animals, is relative. "That which is," says the Preacher, "is far off, and deep, very deep; who can find it out?" (7:24). Even though a wise person claims to know, he or she cannot find it out (8:17). The only thing we know is that we know we do not know. "I know that I know nothing," said Socrates.[3]

The word Koheleth uses for this dismal condition in which we all exist is "vanity." Death makes all things vain. "The word . . . denotes a breath," writes a translator, "exhaled air that disappears."[4] Over half its occurrences in the Bible are in Ecclesiastes. "It is the equivalent of the name of the first man in the Bible to die, Abel; and this may be no accident."[5] Because of death, everything adds up to nothing. There is no ultimate meaning. "Vanity of vanities, says the Preacher, vanity of vanities! All is vanity . . . and a striving after wind" (1:2,14). "Everything . . . is vanity, since one fate comes to all, to the righteous and the wicked, to the good and the evil, to the clean and the unclean . . . . One fate comes to all" (9:1-3). "What advantage [then] has the wise [person] over the fool?" (6:8).

II

If the first thing empiricists do is to examine the evidence, the second thing they do is to develop a working hypothesis. Admittedly this is difficult when the evidence is murky, but there are only two alternatives. One is to give up, the other to go on. Koheleth chose the latter. And I would hazard the guess that that is why he got into the Bible. He got in because he did not blink the facts, even the fact of death. He was rigorously honest. He said what he saw.

The gift of death appears to be that the thought of dying gets us to enjoy life.

But plenty of people have done that. I think he is in the Bible because he had the courage to say what he did *not* see, to move beyond reason to faith, beyond empiricism to hypothesis, beyond seeing to seeing beyond, beyond sensing to imagining. He did so in two ways.

First, he enjoyed life. He hypothesized at least proximate if not ultimate meaning in a life lived to the full. "Life," said Robert Louis Stevenson, "should go down foaming in full body over the precipice." And he said it, you remember, when he had an incurable disease. I know it is customary to read Ecclesiastes as unrelieved gloom, but there is far more to the canny old preacher than that. Maybe this, apart from his stunning realism, is why the Jews read him on the third day of their Feast of Booths, a time of rejoicing, and why Christians read him in the lectionary on the Sunday after Christmas.

To be sure, the orthodox reason for reading Ecclesiastes at the time of rejoicing is, to quote an expert, "to qualify the cheerfulness of that day with the thought that life and its joys are fleeting and that everything has its time."[6] And neither the Jews, to my knowledge, nor the Christians read the joy parts of Ecclesiastes on their special days. Nevertheless, there may be more here than meets the eye, because when we examine the evidence, as good empiricists, we see that, throughout Ecclesiastes, there are constant admonitions to live, love, laugh and be happy. The gift of death appears to be that the thought of dying gets us to enjoy life.

"Enjoy life," the Preacher writes, "with the wife whom you love" (9:9). You do not find that kind of sentence coming from a dyed-in-the-wool cynic. "I commend enjoyment, for man has no good thing under the sun but to eat, and drink, and enjoy himself" (8:15). There may be no ultimate meaning, but there is plenty of proximate. "Go, eat your bread with enjoyment, and drink your wine with a merry heart" (9:7). You do not get a sentence like that from a curmudgeon. "There is nothing better for a man than that he should eat and drink, and find enjoyment in his toil" (2:24). Talk about a working hypothesis—that is as good an hypothesis as any I know for working, for getting out of bed in the morning and not giving up just because you do not have it all figured out. "We have to take a day at a time," a man in a tough situation said to me, echoing the doctor at my daughter's accident.

*E*ven the eating, drinking and enjoyment are "from the hand of God," for apart from God who can eat, drink and enjoy?

To be sure, Koheleth's sentence is gloomy, too. You might as well go ahead and eat and drink and have fun on your job, he says, since there is nothing better to do. But that was his temperament, for one thing, and, for another the sentence is there, and the same sentiment keeps appearing in page after page. It would not keep poking its head through the mass of skepticism if he did not believe it as a working hypothesis. And again, how else do you explain why the book was put into the Bible if it is simply unrelieved Pyrrhonism?

Yes, Koheleth ridicules his own proximate meaning. "I said to myself, 'Come now, I will make a test of pleasure; enjoy yourself.' But behold, this also was vanity" (2:1). As was his toil (2:11). But again and again he comes back to it. Even if eating and drinking and enjoying your job are making the best of a bad situation they are still making the best of a bad situation and therefore to be commended, if not with exuberance—because skeptics are rarely exuberant—at least with honesty and integrity. The gift of death is that it motivates us to enjoy life.

When all the other teachers of the day were teaching duty, obedience, and discipline, the Preacher was teaching his pupils how to rejoice.[7] The others were talking about devoting themselves to hard work, the Puritan ethic— much of which is good, but much of which is less good when it gets in the way of rejoicing. Puritans were not noted for their ability to rejoice.

The Proverbs' writers were talking, in effect, about making an idol of responsibility. How many times have our children heard us tell them to "be responsible"? To be sure, responsibility is a fine quality, but not at the expense of rejoicing. "Rejoice, O young [person] in your youth." He did not have to say that. "And let your heart cheer you in the days of your youth; walk in the ways of your heart and the sight of your eyes" (11:9). "Walk in the ways of your heart!" This from the man who lived in his head, the supreme rationalist in the Bible! Is it any accident that his name was a feminine in the Hebrew?[8] Is it any accident that wisdom is a woman in Proverbs, a woman in Greek? When a man gets in touch with the woman within, then he becomes wise, his head gets in touch with his heart, his intellect with his feelings. All marriage enrichment and *koinonia* groups try to do is get us off our heads and onto our hearts. "Walk in the ways of your heart." "Enjoy life with the wife whom you love." "Eat your bread with enjoyment, and drink your wine with a merry heart."

* * *

The other hypothesis this old empiricist made was that there *is* ultimate meaning after all—namely God. "Remember *also* your Creator in the days of your youth" (12:1). Yes, he puts it immediately before his allegory of advancing years. But he does hypothesize God even if he does not understand God. "Go, eat your bread with enjoyment, and drink your wine with a merry heart; for God has already approved what you do" (9:7). Extraordinary! Even the eating, drinking and enjoyment are "from the hand of God," for apart from God who can eat, drink and enjoy (2:24,25)? Amazing! The *gift* of death is that it is giving us God.

"[God] has made everything beautiful in its time" (3:11). That is quite a statement from an empiricist. You cannot prove it. Indeed, all the evidence appears to be to the contrary. Remember, "the race is not to the swift, nor the battle to the strong, nor bread to the wise, nor riches to the intelligent, nor favor to the men of skill" (9:11). But the race and the bread and all are not to be despised. The material world is good. It is Genesis 1 all over again. What happens in your life is good. "I have seen the business that God has given to the sons of men to be busy with. He has made everything beautiful" (3:10,11). It reminds us of the kaleidoscope mentioned earlier.

To be sure, God's ways are inscrutable. "As you do not know how the spirit comes to the bones in the womb of a woman with child, so you do not know the work of God who makes everything" (11:5). But it is *God* who makes everything. This is quite an hypothesis that the Preacher's negative emotion of melancholy in the face of death is moving him to make! And just because God's ways are inscrutable does not mean they are not beautiful. He has merged the Greek Beauty with the Hebraic Good. Again and again his heart merges with his head, and it is beautiful. The gift of his obsession with death is that it enhances the beauty of life. It brings him more, if not the rest, of who he is.

It not only moves the Preacher beyond reason to faith

in the beautiful as an expression of God; it also moves him to faith in life after death as an expression of God. The good that he sees in eating and drinking and working seems to survive. It is God's gift that everyone should eat and drink and take pleasure in their toil. "I know," he writes, "that whatever God does endures forever" (3:14). You cannot prove that. It is a stunning hypothesis, and it comes after, and in spite of, his rigorous examination of the evidence. We go to our "eternal home" (12:5). Incredible from someone who has only just said that God has put eternity into our minds, "yet *so that [we] cannot* find out what God has done" (3:11).

But Koheleth has found out something that he did not know he knew. "The spirit returns to God who gave it" (12:7). This from someone who had just written, "Who knows whether the spirit of a man goes upward and the spirit of the beast goes down to the earth?" (3:21). *He* knows.

His head battles with his heart to the end. He no sooner says that the spirit returns to God who gave it and so beats death than he ends where he began, by saying, "Vanity of vanities, says the Preacher; all is vanity" (12:8). The empiricist has to have the last word. But the last word, of course, is not vanity but God. "I know that it will be well," he says, "with those who [reverence] God" (8:12). Because for them God has, indeed, "made everything beautiful in its time" (3:11). The skeptic in us, all along, was the man or woman of faith. Irony of ironies, all is irony.

Notes
1. W. Reichert and A. Cohen in A. Cohen, *Soncino Books of the Bible: Ecclesiastes* (London: Soncino, 1969), p. 104.
2. J. Hempel, quoted by O.S. Rankin in *The Interpreter's Bible* (New York: Abingdon, 1956), vol. 5, p. 4.

3. O. Bauernfeind in G. Kittel, *Theological Dictionary of the New Testament* (Grand Rapids, MI: Eerdmans, 1967), vol. 4, p. 521.
4. H.H. Guthrie in *The Interpreter's One-Volume Commentary on the Bible* (New York: Abingdon, 1971), p. 320.
5. Ibid., pp. 320-321.
6. O.S. Rankin, Idem.
7. J.C. Rylaarsdam in *The Layman's Bible Commentary* (Richmond, Va: Knox, 1964), vol. 10, p. 131.
8. O.S. Rankin, op. cit., p. 3.

THE TREASURES OF SELFISHNESS

20

THE GIFT
OF EGO

The call came in the middle of the night. He told me how his two brothers and sister had died. He told me of his long struggle for faith. "I want to learn how to trust," he said. "To let go." And then he added, "I can't seem to trust enough. I can't seem to heal myself."

* * *

The call came for Jesus in the middle of the night. It was a Pharisee named Nicodemus. He came under cover of night so as not to be seen. He came out of his long struggle for faith. Jesus told him he must be born again (John

3:7). "How can this be?" he asked. "Are you a teacher of Israel," Jesus asked, "and yet you do not understand this?" (John 3:10).

Do I surrender or am I surrendered? Do I let go or am I pulled away? Do I accept Christ as my Lord and Savior or am I accepted? Do I believe or am I brought to belief? Do we choose God or does God choose us? Is faith a work or is faith a gift? "I don't believe in miracles," a man said to me coming out of church. "I believe in hard work."

I

Hard work can be the last refuge of the ego. Ego in this sense is egotism. Hard work has worked in every other aspect of life, and we are egotistical enough to assume that it will work in religion. We give it all we have, as the man on the telephone. We go to the people we think have the answers, as Nicodemus to Jesus. We pull out the books and go to the Bible studies and join the prayer groups and the *koinonia* groups. We even put our faith into action through a multitude of good works. Whatever it takes, we will "bind" *ourselves* "back" to who we are. *We* will do it, which is works, rather than allowing God to do it, which is grace.

The only trouble is, our own religious work doesn't seem to work. We are like the man on the telephone with three loved ones gone and old age haunting him saying, "I can't trust enough." We are like Nicodemus coming to Jesus because, even though we are Pharisees and have observed all the formalities of our religion, we still can't trust enough. We are like the man coming out of church who has risen to the zenith of his career and who steadfastly refuses to believe in miracles because to believe in a miracle is to say that God does it, I don't, and that is the one thing I cannot say because I believe in hard work.

And that is fine, make no mistake, as far as it goes. The gift of ego is to get us to recognize the limits of ego. The man coming out of church *is* in church, an organization dedicated to the limits of ego. And he is there not because he comes but because he is drawn. Something is going on in him that pulls him away from his Sunday paper.

Faith is not a work. It is the hard work that does not work. It is a gift. A miracle. A grace.

The gift of hard work is that it gets us to recognize the limits of hard work. This does not mean the hard work should not be done. Indeed, it has to be done in order for us to realize the limits of what we can do. We have to attack our religion with the same zeal we bring to our jobs and homes and schools. That is what Nicodemus did. He gave it all he had. He even risked his professional status. He put himself on the line, like the man on the telephone. Paul gave it all he had, only to realize that he didn't have enough. *Then* the miracle occurred and Jesus came. *He* didn't come to Jesus. He was doing all his hard work on an entirely different track. Jesus came to him. But not until the hard work had gone on for years. The gift of ego was that it brought him to the limits of ego.

The "limits of ego" is a phrase for a word, and the word is one we encountered in chapter 17, "The Gift of Chance," namely, *need*. The only way we can "come to Jesus" is out of need. It comes from the root "to be exhausted" and "die." To come to the limits of ego and so

be open to faith is to become exhausted with the hard
work of searching for God. It is to die to the old self, the
hard-work self, and to rise to the new self, the worked-
upon self. "You must be born anew," Jesus said to Nicodemus (John 3:7).

It is the great passive statement of the Bible. Faith is
not a work. It is the hard work that does not work. It is a
gift. A miracle. A grace. We were given life. We had nothing to do with our own conceptions. It is the same with the
life of faith. Faith is the last refuge of the ego—only for the
ego to find it is the one place where work does not work.
We have to die to the old self and be raised to the new.

II

So what do we have to do to get faith? We have to do the
hardest work of all. We have to confess. Only *we* will not
do it. We *cannot* do it. It is too hard. That is why, when it *is*
done, we say God did it. Our confession is God speaking
through us. "I can will what is right," Paul said, "but I cannot do it" (Rom. 7:18). "Who will deliver me from this
body of death? Thanks be to God" (Rom. 7:24,25).

Confession is an old word for saying what our needs
are. And we only need when we have, as we say,
exhausted our own resources. "When I am weak," an
exhausted Paul confessed, "then I am strong" (2 Cor.
12:10). It was the basis of all Jesus' talk about the humble
people. In many churches, the first act of worship on Sunday after praising God is for the congregation to humble
themselves, to confess their needs, to raise up to God the
limits of the ego's hard work.

But confession is hard. It looks weak, helpless. It is so
unlike us. So out of control. So irrational. What will our

children think? To show weakness to our children! To our parents! I heard a psychiatrist on the radio talking about workaholics. They are still trying to please their parents, he said. Somehow they got the idea that their parents would love them only if they worked hard. So we have all these workaholics, he said, who cannot even take time for a walk in the woods because they never did when they were young, and now they are afraid to. Will I get back on time? Will I even get there? Should I take an umbrella? Will there be bears? It reminds me of a friend who was upset that her son was spending all his time after school and even during the summer in a myriad of activities and so had no time to "sit under a tree." The force of his egotistical subculture was that great.

"I believe in hard work," a recovering alcoholic says, "but I also believe in miracles." It was hard work that brought him to the point where he could see that his work would not work. Then, at the point of his need, at the point of the death of the old life, he was born again to a new one, and he is not afraid to use the word "miracle." He is a successful businessman, and he is not embarrassed when he uses the word "miracle." I have even heard him, looking back, call his alcoholism a "gift." It brought him closer to the rest of who he was, closer to God.

Job was a good man. But Job had a problem—his ego. He did everything right. He even believed right. He honestly believed he was a good man. And he was. His problem was that he had not yet shared his need on his knees. So God was going to have to confront him with reality. God was going to have to bring him to faith—not as the last refuge of the ego but as the first cry of new birth. First the tears of helplessness. Then the tears of joy. Our tears are bringing us God. God comes to us in our tears. "I had not cried since I was ten years old," my recovering friend said. Job lost his health. He lost his wealth. He lost his family. Finally, he had a need. Then he had a faith.

The man on the telephone will never break through to what Job and Paul "moved out" to until he is exhausted by his furious fight for faith and finds himself on his knees confessing his need.

It was hard work in prospect; it was no work in retrospect. It was all a matter of will in prospect; it was being willed in retrospect. It was ego, me, I will believe, in prospect; it was God, Jesus, in retrospect. "If anyone is in Christ," Paul wrote, "he is a new creation . . . . All this is from God" (2 Cor. 5:17,18). "Work out your own salvation," we have seen him write. That's ego. That's hard work. "For God is at work in you" (Phil. 2:12,13). That's gift. That's not hard work. "They are justified by his grace as a *gift*," he said (Rom. 3:24). And he said this as a Pharisee, a No. 1 self-helper. "Christ Jesus has made me his own" (Phil. 3:12). Note the passive. He did not do it. He did not make himself a Christian. Christ did. Christ met him at the point of his need. "I have been crucified with Christ; it is no longer I who live, but Christ who lives in me" (Gal. 2:20).

Faith is passive. We think it is active, but the only faith we get out of that is belief in hard work and ego and our own goodness. For many this is a necessary step in the process of faith, but the man on the telephone will never break through to what Job and Paul "moved out" to until he is exhausted by his furious fight for faith and finds himself on his knees confessing his need. "I know a man in Christ who fourteen years ago was caught up to the third heaven," Paul wrote. "On behalf of *this* man I will boast, but on my own behalf I will not boast, except of my weaknesses" (2 Cor. 12:2,5). Because it is our weaknesses that are bringing us strength. Faith is the announcement that *I* cannot do it. That my ego is not sufficient. That I cannot control this particular aspect of my life. It is driving me to believe. It is forcing me to believe. It is weakening me to believe. I *need* to believe.

III

You know it's faith when you find yourself confessing. You also know it's faith when you find yourself loving. When you strip away the cliché, to love means to be with others in *their* exhaustion. It is what people of faith do. It is the purest form of evangelism. It means to be present with them at their rebirth from death. When people give you the gift of their tears, it is a precious gift. It means they are making their confession to you. You are there at their birth into new life. Jesus was there for Nicodemus. And at the end Nicodemus was there for Jesus. It was Nicodemus who came with a hundred pounds of spices to anoint the body of Jesus. He had passed from hard work through need to love. His faith was now being proved by his work (John 19:39).

I do not have faith if I do not have love. The journey inward must always be accompanied by the journey outward. "Faith without works is dead," we read in James 2:26 *(KJV)*. That is the point of the mission emphasis in churches—to be there for people wherever they are, in their needs, sharing their tears, beyond our egos to theirs. "Bear one another's burdens," wrote a loving Paul, "and so fulfil the law of Christ" (Gal. 6:2). That kind of love is the result of faith, just as faith is the result of grace. "Faith is our response to God's grace," Luther said. "Faith working through love," Paul said (Gal. 5:6). I will not be moved to be beside someone in his or her tears unless I feel that God is beside me in mine. "We love because [God] first loved us" (1 John 4:19). Love happens as I weep with somebody else the fierce tears that come from the frustration of going up against the limits of my ego and so finding that "faith depends," as Paul put it, "not upon [our] will or exertion, but upon God's mercy" (Rom. 9:16).

"By his great mercy" wrote an astonished Peter, "we have been born anew to a living hope" (1 Pet. 1:3). There it is again, the great passive act of faith. That is why the first Christians referred to themselves as slaves. As we have seen, it was the most common word they used to describe themselves (Titus 1:1; Jas. 1:1, *et. pas.*). It was an epitome of the passive, of what had been done through them rather than by them, of the miracle which came on the other side of hard work, of exhaustion, of death. "By grace," early Christians were taught, "you have been saved through faith; and this is *not* your own doing, it is the *gift* of God—*not* because of works, lest any [one] should boast. For we are [God's] workmanship" (Eph. 2:8-10). In the words of an exhausted Paul, "When we cry 'Abba! Father!' it is the Spirit" (Rom. 8:15,16).

21
THE GIFT
OF PRIDE

He had to have it all before he hit forty. It was important to him to have made his mark by then. Honor after honor came his way, promotion after promotion. He never thought twice about it. It was just something you did. You achieved. You were successful. You made your contribution. Sure, it took long hours. Sure, some sacrifices had to be made. But that was life. Welcome to reality.

Then he got divorced.

A number of us wondered what was pushing him so. His parents? His siblings? His peers? But they were all outside. What was goading him on the inside? Where had he gotten the idea that he was what he did rather than did

what he was? Was it the early grading in school? Football?
The culture? But again, they were outside. Where did this
hunger for making a name for himself come from on the
inside? Was it how he would become immortal? Was this
how he would beat death?

When we talked I saw all the earmarks of a classical
narcissist. He was self-centered, arrogant, grandiose, had
a hard time entertaining other points of view, and he could
not understand how there might be more to life than
climbing the corporate ladder.

Now, of course, thanks to his divorce, he was starting
at the bottom again—if he could see it that way. I must
confess that I was not at all hopeful that he could, that he
would ever see it for the disaster it was. But you never
know.

* * *

I

The disaster came about, according to the story of the
tower of Babel, because of pride (Gen. 11:1-9). To be
sure, there is a positive side to pride. There was nothing
"intrinsically wrong" with pride for the ancient Hebrews,
we are told by the experts.[1] There is what we call "pardonable pride" in a job well done, a good report card, a
happy home. For the ancient Jews there was pride in their
land (Isa. 4:2), as we have in ours, pride in their city (Isa.
60:14), as we have in our cities. And so on. But that is not
the pride the story is talking about.

The story is talking about the pride that gets out of

hand. That, of course, is the trouble with pride. It can get out of hand fast, and what was once pardonable becomes questionable. The ancient Jews told the story of how the tower was built, how it was built for a good purpose, the unification of the races, but how something went wrong.

"Let us make a name for ourselves," the tower builders said (Gen. 11:4). That was what went wrong. It affected everything they did. It turned their altruism into egotism and their egotism into chaos. Their language was confused. We call it "babble" from Babel. Their homelands were diffused. They were scattered over the world. We are back where we started with Noah and the flood, Adam and Eve, the chaotic creation of the world.

My name. My family. My company. My community. My school. My country. My job. All are an extension of me. They are how I wrest my immortality from the gods.

The source of the story was the ancient cuneiform literature. It came from the story of the building of Babylon and its temple.[2] And that again would be only of academic interest if it were not for the fact that the story traveled from land to land until it reached Israel,[3] which implies universality—the story rivets our attention because it applies to us. We are out there building our towers. We are building monuments to ourselves. "Let us make a name for ourselves" is every bit as much our watchword as theirs. If we strip it all away and get down to the bottom line of motivation for much of our creativity we will see, at its rawest, that our motivation is egotism. My name. My family. My company. My community. My school. My country. My job. All are an extension of me. They are how I wrest my immortality from the gods.

What could be nobler than the unification of the races? Of my family? My community? What could be nobler than making my business as large and efficient as possible so that I can give jobs to people who need them, put bread on people's tables, roofs over people's heads, and pay taxes to care for the destitute? I'm building my tower, and all for the betterment of humanity.

"I abhor the pride of Jacob," says the Lord (Amos 6:8). "Behold, I will profane my sanctuary, the pride of your power, the delight of your eyes, and the desire of your soul" (Ezek. 24:21). The Hebrew root for pride meant "to be high," "to be lifted up," "to tower."[4]

> The Lord of hosts has a day
>   against all that is proud and lofty,
>   against all that is lifted up and high;
> against all the cedars of Lebanon,
>   lofty and lifted up;
>   and against all the oaks of Bashan;
> against all the high mountains,
>   and against all the lofty hills;
> against every high tower,
>   and against every fortified wall;
> against all the ships of Tarshish,
>   and against all the beautiful craft.
> And the haughtiness of [the people] shall be
>   humbled,
>   and the pride of [the people] shall be
>   brought low;
>   and the Lord alone will be exalted in that day
> (Isa. 2:12-17).

II

The ancient Jews looked around them at the empirical data. They saw nationalism. They saw war. They saw individualism. They saw hate. The hand which held the olive branch also held the sword. To be sure, they saw the good, too. That is why their first story was of the goodness of creation. But they also saw the bad, and they had to explain it. Where did the bad come from? It came from us. We had overreached.

The tower was built so high in the story that, like a child's tower of blocks, it fell. We have discovered the fall of humanity. Adam and Eve overreached. Icarus flew so high his wings melted, and he fell to his death. The root of the word for pride in the Greek was "trespass,"[5] "encroachment,"[6] "an act which invades the sphere of another to [the other's] hurt."[7] The high ones, the lofty ones, the towering ones had invaded the sphere of God.

There was another myth in Greece at the same time the story of the tower of Babel was making the rounds in Palestine. It was of Prometheus, the titan who stole fire from the gods. Ever since, the word "Promethean" has stood for "boldly creative"[8] tower-building. The only trouble is that we tend to forget what happened to Prometheus. For his act of titanic defiance, of encroachment, of lofty trespass, he was condemned by the gods to permanent torture. Just as we are punished by the law of the state when we trespass on property, so we are punished by the law of God when we trespass on God.

Is it any wonder the word for "holy" in the Hebrew included the concept of distance?[9] The builders of the tower of Babel sought to overcome the distance between God and us, rather than let God overcome it. Prometheus tried to do the same.

Every day we are seeking to overcome the distance. It is highly imaginative, boldly creative activity. The only trouble is, it is not imaginative enough. It is not creative enough. We are mesmerized by our success and cannot imagine the creative process going on *through* us rather than *by* us. *We* built the tower, not God. *We* built the company, not God. *We* built the happy home, not God. We are so dazzled by our achievements that we can no longer see God. "We take away the mystery," someone said to me. "We take all the apples off the tree."

Pride is the inability to keep on imagining. Pride is stopping short. Pride is saying the distance is overcome when, in fact, the distance has never been greater. Pride is the inability to imagine that there is more to life than what I build. The ancient Hebrews looked around themselves at the empirical data of egotism and egotism squared, or nationalism, and they explained it by saying we had overreached. They saw the confusion of languages and diffusion of races, and they explained it as the result of trespass, of invading the sphere of God.

III

The *gift* of pride is that it brings us God. Whenever you feel confused, look for the source of your confusion. It may well be your pride, not in the positive but in the presumptuous sense. Whenever you feel diffused, all over the place, "spacey," as we say, it may be the fall of your achievement tower, your control tower, bringing you closer to God. Indeed, God *is* what comes to us in our confusion and diffusion. That is not all God is, but God is at least that. Is it any wonder that a later Jewish book, the book of Jubilees, called the tower of Babel "Catastrophe" (Jub. 10:26)?[10] Far from running from such catastrophes in our lives, as the self-help books suggest, we should welcome them as God's toppling of the tower of pride in order to come to us. God comes "down" to us. We do not go "up" to God. That is the point of the Incarnation, as opposed to the ziggurat. You climbed up the seven stories of the ziggurat, and the gods walked down.[11] In the Incarnation, God came "down," to a stable. There was no climb on our part.

God comes to us not only in our mountaintop experiences but also in our bottom-land experiences. Not only in our peak experiences, as the psychologist Maslow puts it, but also in our valley experiences. Indeed, the peak becomes a peak only as it rises from the valley. It is in my confusion about my family and where I am going in my life that I am being brought to God. It is in my diffusion, being all over the place in my job and unable to concentrate at school, that *God* is being incarnated. I am being "bound back" to the rest of who I am.

If, that is, I will go on imagining. The trouble is that when I have created something, I stop imagining. I turn the thing I have imagined into existence—that is, the thing I have created—into what the ancient Hebrews called an idol. The tower I have built so imaginatively—in my job or home or school—becomes an end in itself rather than a means to a greater end. I step back and look at my splendid record and say, "Wow! That's me." When I should keep on imagining and say, "That's God."

In Florence, Italy, in the church just up from Ghiberti's famous doors, you will find Michelangelo's slave, an astonishing sculpture done toward the end of his life. He was so proud of his achievement, the story goes, that he took a sledgehamer and broke his creation's arm. He had gotten

too close, he felt, to perfection. He had overcome too
much distance. He had trespassed on God. Retribution in
the form of confusion and diffusion is essential to preserve
distance. Nemesis always goes with hubris. [12]

> Their land is filled with idols;
>> they bow down to the work of their hands,
>> to what their own fingers have made.
> So [we are] humbled,
>> and . . . brought low (Isa. 2:8,9).

The word "idol" in English comes ultimately from the
root for "see." When we imagine an image into creative
existence, we are tempted to stop seeing. We are so
excited by the "form," the word in Greek from which we
get our word "idol," that we miss the substance. We are
so thrilled by what we have done that we miss the God
behind what we have done. We cannot see through our
achievements to what has been achieved through us.
Imagination is seeing through. Pride is not seeing through.
Pride is viewing our towers as opaque. Imagination is
viewing our towers as glass. Pride is viewing our towers
as mirrors. Imagination is viewing our towers as panes.

The reason presumptuous pride is a sin in the Bible is
that, among other things, it kills the imagination. It kills
the image of God. The ego thinks it owns God when in
reality God owns the ego. I do not fully control my imagination. The images that come to me are God coming to
me. What's to lose from using that as an hypothesis? When
I am confused, the images coming to me, like falling towers, are God coming to me. When I am diffused and all
over the place, the images coming to me, like ancient zig-
gurats with their tops in the heavens falling down, are God
coming to me.

Noah walked with God. The reason he could handle the flood was that he knew God was handling him. No one else knew that. That is why they drowned. America is becoming increasingly secularized. We no longer see the God behind the achievement. The company, the family, the church become idols. We crowd each other. We take each other's space. We trespass.

In the brokenness is the healing, in the fall the rise, in the confusion the still small voice, and in the diffusion the many mansions of the house of God.

This is what happens when we kill the imagination. We no longer see God behind our achievements. The Bible gives us an opportunity to demonstrate that we see *through* our achievements, that we are building the Kingdom of God as well as our own kingdom, that we are being Hebraic as well as Promethean.

Only we do not always take that opportunity. We are like King Uzziah in the Bible.

> And he built towers in the wilderness, and hewed out many cisterns, . . . and he had farmers and vinedressers in the hills and in the fertile lands, for he loved the soil . . . . In Jerusalem he made engines, invented by skilful men, to be on the towers and the corners, to shoot arrows and great stones. And his fame spread far, for he was marvelously helped, till he was strong. But *when he was strong he grew*

proud,   to   his   destruction   (2   Chron.
26:10,15,16).

Pride goes before destruction, and a haughty
spirit before a fall (Prov. 16:18). A man's pride
will bring him low (29:23).

The *gift* of pride is that it brings us low. It brings us
God, whom we often see better from depths than from
heights. The *gift* of pride is that when we no longer understand each other or ourselves, when we babble and are
confused, when we no longer want to be with each other
or with ourselves, and are thrown out of our space as
Adam and Eve and Noah out of theirs, and are proudly
scattered, in the imaginations of our hearts (Luke 1:51),
and are diffused—*that* is when we begin to see God
because at last we see *through* ourselves.

In the words of Ezekiel, who said that the temple towers had to fall because of pride: *"Then* you will know that I
am the Lord God" (Ezek. 24:24). After the fall, because of
the fall, during the confusion and diffusion, that is when we
can imagine God. That is when the images that come to us
are images of God. In the brokenness is the healing, in the
fall the rise, in the confusion the still small voice, and in the
diffusion the many mansions of the house of God.

Notes
1. G. Bertram in G. Kittel, *Theological Dictionary of the Old Testament* (Grand Rapids, Mich.: Eerdmans, 1972), vol. 8, p. 299.
2. E.A. Speiser, "Genesis," in *The Anchor Bible* (New York: Doubleday, 1964), vol. 1, p. 75.
3. J. Skinner, "Genesis," in *The International Critical Commentary* (Edinburgh: Clark, 1956), vol. 1, p. 228.
4. J.A. Wharton in *The Interpreter's Dictionary of the Bible* (New York: Abingdon, 1962), vol. 3, p. 876.
5. Bertram, op. cit., p. 295.

6. Ibid., p. 297.
7. Ibid., p. 295.
8. *American Heritage Dictionary* (New York: Random, 1969).
9. J. Muilenberg in *The Interpreter's Dictionary of the Bible,* vol. 2, pp. 617, 619.
10. Skinner, op. cit., p. 224.
11. Ibid., p. 226.
12. "The gods as bearers of nemesis oppose [humanity's] hubris with retribution," Bertram, op. cit., p. 297.

22
THE GIFT OF SIN

The problem is that she doesn't like herself and is projecting it onto her husband in the form of anger. But the anger
is at herself for not liking herself. If she liked herself, she
wouldn't have to take anything out on him. What is happening is that her anger is a cover for fear. She is afraid to
look at herself, to confront herself with the facts about
herself, and then gradually begin to like herself better.
What she needs, in a word, is to feel forgiven.

Maybe that's why she's here, in a church. I have a
hunch that she knows the forgiveness is here. If only she
can access it. She comes to church regularly, and I see her
tormented face before me as I enter the pulpit. But she is

not in one of our small groups yet, which is too bad. Because it is there that she might experience the forgiveness she needs. The others in the group would tell her she is forgiven. They would make the announcement to her. They would be Jesus for her.

Of course, we are all in the same position she is, to one degree or another. We may not project our dislike of ourselves onto others in anger, but we may project it in any number of other ways. Any way you look at it, we still have to deal with the basic problem, that of having done things we don't like ourselves for.

One way to solve the problem is through self-help, which my iron-willed friend is employing at the moment. Like the woman in the preface, she reads all the self-help books. I don't want to criticize such measures—unless they are the only measures.

Another way to solve the problem of doing things we don't like ourselves for doing or having done is through divine help, which complements the self-help and carries us the rest of the way to integrated living. To get the rest of the way, to reach original blessing as a complement to original sin, we could well use the Christian gospel.

And what is the gospel? We are sinners. We need a savior. His name is Jesus.

* * *

I

We have suggested that sin is self-reliance. It is thinking I can bind myself back to the rest of who I am. It is applying rational, can-do, frontier individualism, which may work for 49 percent of life—instead of applying irrational, can't-do transcendentalism—to the 51 percent of life where self-sufficiency does not work.

If the Bible says anything, it says we cannot achieve our own wholeness. "I can will what is right," we have seen Paul say, "but I cannot do it . . . . Who will deliver me from this body of death?" (Rom. 7:18,24). He needed a savior. He could not save himself.

The ancient Hebrews' most profound word for sin was "rebellion."[1] "Sins of all kinds," writes an expert, "were rightly interpreted as, first of all, sins against God."[2] "Against thee, thee only, have I sinned," wrote the psalmist (51:4). Therefore sin was far more than the violation of an external code. It was whatever went against our internal grain. Sin is whatever I do that is like chalk pushed the wrong way across a blackboard.

Jesus repristinated this ancient idea of sin, saving it from the externalists, the legalists, who were saying that so long as you lived right you *were* right. Jesus saw deeper. "From within," he said, "out of the heart . . . come evil thoughts" (Mark 7:21). "The heart is deceitful above all things," the Bible had said, "and desperately corrupt" (Jer. 17:9). "Every imagination of the thoughts of [their hearts] was only evil continually" (Gen. 6:5).

That does not appear to be much of a gift, but it is the Judeo-Christian doctrine of original sin, an idea that has been massively forgotten by the self-help books and modern humanistic psychology. Indeed, it is the reverse of what we normally hear, which is all sorts of variations on the theme of the perfectibility of humanity being played by the pop psychologists, none of whom ever uses the word sin, which, we have seen, comes from the root for "be" and is the very essence of our being, hence "original."

II

Where is the *gift* in sin? The gift is that it throws us off our own resources and onto God's. We are sinners. We need a savior. We cannot save ourselves. The more we try the more we fail, as Paul found out. It only plunged him deeper into self-righteousness and Pharisaism.

There was nothing Paul could do except do everything he could because only *then* would he realize there was nothing he could do. It had to *be* done *for* him. "Who will deliver *me*?" The reason John the Baptist's father was deaf and mute was to emphasize his dependence (Luke 1:20). It was a graphic image of passivity. We are sinners. We need a savior. We cannot save ourselves.

It is when Zechariah writes the word "John," which means "gift of God," that he hears and speaks (Luke 1:63,64). It is when we realize that we are in the 51 percent of life which we cannot control but which controls us that we can hear and speak of salvation. The blind see. The deaf hear. The mute talk. That is how they know I am the Christ, Jesus said (Luke 7:22).

The key word in what John's father Zechariah says is forgiveness (Luke 1:77). It is arguably the most important word in the Bible with the possible exception of "cannot" as in "I can will what is right but I cannot do it." When I can't get my act together, when I can't become the person I was meant to be, when I can't get the A, can't get the promotion, can't get along with my spouse, can't even like myself as much as I would like to, can't stop rebelling against myself—that is when I need to experience forgiveness, and that is when forgiveness can be there. It is forgiveness that gives us the 51 percent dimension of self.

"I will forgive their iniquity, and I will remember their sin no more" (Jer. 31:34). The gift of sin is that it gives us

God. What greater gift could there be? It was the gift John was announcing. "You, child, will be called the prophet of the Most High; . . . to give knowledge of salvation to [God's] people in the forgiveness of their sins" (Luke 1:76,77).

But how do I *receive* the gift? Only when I need it. When do I need it? Only when I am convinced of my sin. When am I convinced of my sin? Only when I discover what I cannot do. When do I discover that? When I come up against something in my life that is too big for me to handle. When does that happen? Maybe not for a long time.

"It doesn't happen all at once," the nursery horse says in *The Velveteen Rabbit*. "You become. It takes a long time." "Does it hurt?" asks the Rabbit. "Sometimes," says the Skin Horse.

> [But] when you are real you don't mind being hurt . . . . Generally, by the time you are real, most of your hair has been loved off, and your eyes drop out and you get loose in the joints and very shabby. But these things don't matter at all, because once you are Real you can't be ugly, except to people who don't understand.[3]

III

We are sinners. We need a savior. His name is Jesus. Jesus takes us beyond "can't," across that 2 percent, to limitless "can." God's forgiveness incarnated in Christ gets us over into the 51 percent and begins to open it up. The possibilities are staggering. "Having been set free from sin," Paul exulted (Rom. 6:18), he could now handle anything.

> In toil and hardship, through many a sleepless night, in hunger and thirst, often without food, in cold and exposure. And, apart from other things, there is the daily pressure upon me of my anxiety for all the churches. Who is weak, and I am not weak? (2 Cor. 11:27-29).

I was coming around a corner when the car behind gave me a long horn and screeched past. "Wouldn't it be fun," I said to my wife, "if he got picked up?" We never lose our original sin.

With Jesus the things that are preventing our being the person we were meant to be are sent away. "Send away" is the root of "forgiveness" in both the Hebrew and Greek, the Old Testament and New.[4] The word that John's father used meant to "let go, set aside, leave behind."[5] And what we do when we are "in Christ," as Paul put it, is to leave the old self behind with its roadblocks to being what we were meant to be. We do not leave it completely, which is the point of original sin, but we do leave it behind. I was coming around a corner when the car behind gave me a long horn and screeched past. "Wouldn't it be fun," I said to my wife, "if he got picked up?" We never lose our original sin.

How, then, does a person receive the gift of Christ if that is the key to forgiveness, and if forgiveness is the key

to being the people God meant us to be, the key to being
real, the key to wholeness, to salvation, as John's father
put it? The answer has to be somewhere in the word
"can't." And in a particular implication in the word—
perhaps "hurt." There are many things I cannot do. But
there are only a few things that make me hurt when I cannot do them. This is where we come head-to-head with
Christian realism. John grew up and was killed. Jesus grew
up and was killed. Paul, Stephen, Peter—all the first
Christians knew what it was to follow Christ as ancient
Israel's suffering servants, as pictured in Isaiah 53.

When Ignatius wrote his letters around A.D. 100 to
the tiny churches he passed as he was led away to Rome
as a prisoner by his "Ten Leopards," as he called them, he
wrote this to the church in Smyrna: "To the church of God
which has through mercy obtained every kind of gift,
which is filled with faithful love, and is deficient in no gift."[6]
He could write this kind of thing as he was led to his death.
In another letter he again writes, "The Church which has
had obtained mercy . . . which is beloved."[7]

What is it that you have come up against in your life
that you cannot do, that prevents your becoming the person you were meant to be, and that hurts you? Jesus is
there. Or at least Jesus *can be* there. And until we reach
such a point, the transcendent is often not there, we
haven't entered the 51 percent, and we are not yet fully
real. Jesus came into Paul's life at the point of his need,
where "can" had turned into "can't" and "can't" into hurt
and hurt into forgiveness on the road to Damascus and
then forgiveness into limitless "can."

When he felt forgiven, when the adventure of becoming Paul turned into "mercy," his word and that of Ignatius,
his whole life turned around. Now he could repent. Now
he could accept himself. Now he could forgive. The 2 per-

cent was like the mustard seed, giving him enormous power. Forgiveness is the perfect gift. Why not give it to someone you love but who has hurt you very much— because the God who loves you has given it to you, even though it hurt unbearably, in the gift of a Son?

"Dear Bob," a letter read. "I have had something on my mind for many years now, and that is that, Bob, I need to say 'I'm sorry,' and will you forgive me for my anger? . . . This is long overdue, I'm sorry."

Or, as theologian Reinhold Niebuhr once put it:

> Nothing worth doing is completed in our lifetime; therefore we must be saved by hope. Nothing true or beautiful or good makes complete sense in any immediate context of history; therefore we must be saved by faith. Nothing we do, however virtuous, can be accomplished alone; therefore we are saved by love. No virtuous act is quite as virtuous from the standpoint of our friend or foe as from our standpoint. Therefore we must be saved by the final form of love which is forgiveness.[8]

Notes
1. S.J. DeVries in *The Interpreter's Dictionary of the Bible* (New York: Abingdon, 1962), vol. 3, p. 361.
2. Idem.
3. M. Williams, *The Velveteen Rabbit* (New York: Doubleday, n.d.), p. 17.
4. W.A. Quanbeck, in *The Interpreter's Dictionary of the Bible* (New York: Abingdon, 1962), vol. 1, p. 315.
5. R. Bultmann in G. Kittel, *Theological Dictionary of the New Testament* (Grand Rapids, MI: Eerdmans, 1964), vol. 1, p. 509.
6. Ignatius, "Letter to the Smyrneans," in A. Roberts and J. Donaldson, *The Ante-Nicene Fathers* (Grand Rapids, MI: Wm. B. Eerdmans, 1977), p. 86.
7. Ibid., "Epistle to the Romans," op. cit., p. 73.
8. R. Niebuhr, *The Irony of American History* (New York: Scribner's, 1962), p. 63.

23

THE GIFT OF DESPAIR

"This journey he has been asked to take," she wrote me of her husband, "is incredible. Every system of his body has been affected. Each week seems to bring a new crisis. Three weeks ago a retinal hemorrhage temporarily blinded him in one eye. Two weeks ago he took a nasty fall. He's had to swallow his pride and now uses a walker much of the time. Last week he was involved in yet another car accident—despite using his hand controls.

"There are rare moments of discouragement. 'I guess God didn't want me after all!' But for the most part his acceptance of his lot puts me to shame."

How do people do it? How does he remain so confi-

dent, even optimistic? What is it that keeps him going when every system in his body is shutting down? "I thrive on the prayers of you and the congregation," he writes. "I may be sick, but it's the kind one can cope with." And the way he copes is not only with family and friends but with prayer. His desperate condition has somehow brought him new evidence for God.

It hasn't been easy. "I must confess," he writes, "at times I feel like Job and ask, Why me?" But somehow God keeps breaking through. It is almost as though God breaks through because he is in such desperate straits. Indeed, if he weren't in such straits maybe God wouldn't have broken through as much. You never know. But what you do know is that somehow, in his despair, through his despair, because of his despair, the treasures of darkness are being revealed as never before.

* * *

It is quite possible that any of the negative emotions we have been discussing could plunge us into a situation which seems equally desperate. Perhaps we are in such a situation now. It is like the man in the Bible whose daughter died. He came to Jesus and fell on his knees, desperate with grief (Matt. 9:18). We do not know where to turn. We feel trapped, perhaps even suicidal. "We were so utterly, unbearably crushed," Paul wrote, "that we despaired of life itself" (2 Cor. 1:8). "All the interest of my reason (speculative as well as practical)," said Immanuel Kant, "comes together in the following three questions: (1) What can I know? (2) What ought I to do? (3) What may I hope?"[1]

I

Hope is born of despair, a word whose root means "without hope." Hope begins where we end. When we are driven to our knees, then hope can begin. Our descent to the cross strips us of the very thing we thought we needed most, self-reliance. "Cursed is the [one] who trusts in [humanity]" (Jer. 17:5). Because it is a false trust. There is no final hope in us. They had done everything they could, and the leading citizen's daughter was dead.

The "fall of humanity" is a fall through every level of self-trust. "See the [one] who . . . trusted in the abundance of . . . riches," scoffs the psalmist, "and sought refuge in . . . wealth" (Ps. 52:7). He is laughed at. "The [workers] trust in [their] own creation[s]" (Hab. 2:18). They are scorned. When we trust in our own plans we are frustrated (Ps. 33:10).

Even when we trust in our places of worship we are mocked. "Do not trust in these deceptive words," Jeremiah says sarcastically, "'This is the temple of the Lord, the temple of the Lord, the temple of the Lord'" (Jer. 7:4). It is the same when they put their trust in the pharaoh in Egypt (Isa. 36:4), in the government (Ps. 146:3), in arms (Jer. 5:17; Ps. 33:17), in their own homes (Job 8:15).

> Rise up, you women who are at
>   ease, hear my voice;
>   you complacent daughters, give
>   ear to my speech.
> In little more than a year
>   you will shudder, you complacent
>   women;
> for the vintage will fail,
>   the fruit harvest will not come (Isa.
> 32:9,10).

We must distinguish between proximate and ultimate trust. Every one of the above is fine for proximate trust, but when every one fails in a situation because we despair, because we are driven to our knees in grief or terror, then what? The word for feeling secure in the Old Testament, according to a Bible expert, is "almost always . . . negative . . . when applied to [humanity] and . . . positive . . .

God becomes possible in my despair, where God may have been impossible in my complacency.

---

when applied to God."[2] God alone is our hope, and anything else is idolatrous. More to the point, anything else is hopeless.

> This is the exultant city
>   that dwelt secure,
> that said to herself,
>   "I am and there is none else."
> What a desolation she has become,
>   a lair for wild beasts!
> Everyone who passes by her
>   hisses and shakes his fist (Zeph. 2:15).

When I come to the end of my rope, I come to the beginning of God. Not inevitably, of course, but possibly. God becomes possible in my despair, where God may have been impossible in my complacency. The thing that drives me to my knees is the very thing that is bringing me

God. That is why we can call it a gift. "We were so utterly, unbearably crushed that we despaired of life itself. Why," Paul continued, "we felt that we had received the sentence of death; but that was to make us rely *not* on ourselves but on God" (2 Cor. 1:8,9).

II

If hope begins in despair it continues in patience. The only way I am ever going to see God in my despair is to wait. "Wait for the Lord" (Ps. 27:14). "Be still, and know that I am God" (Ps. 46:10). "Patience" comes from the root for "suffer." We suffer as we wait for the rest of who we are to be revealed, as we move from proximate to ultimate security. But that is all right. It is the process by which God comes. It is why the cross is the most universal symbol. It symbolizes the suffering needed to open up the rest of who we are. Look at Paul's explanation of the process. It is one of the most hopeful sentences in the Bible.

> We rejoice in our sufferings, knowing that suffering produces endurance, and endurance produces character, and character produces hope, and hope does not disappoint us, because God's love has been poured into our hearts through the Holy Spirit which has been given to us (Rom. 5:3-5).

The thing that causes our suffering is also causing our endurance, which is bringing us hope. "Endurance" is one of the key words in the New Testament. It meant to expe-

rience something that has come against our will, like the
sting of grief, the shock of battle, the coming of death.[3]
Around 200 B.C. it came to mean "spiritual staying
power," which later enabled people to go to their deaths
for Jesus.[4] It was that powerful, that productive of hope.
"Here is a call," wrote the Revelation writer at a time of
intense persecution, "for the endurance . . . of the saints"
(Rev. 13:10). As he continues the description of his vision,
he repeats the call (see 14:12). "[The one] who endures to
the end will be saved," Jesus says (Matt. 10:22), shortly
after He heals the man's daughter. Indeed, a later Christian was to call endurance "the queen of virtues."[5] Why?
Because it enables us to "see" God. In our despair, if we
will wait, we are opened to God. It is like a time exposure.
The lens is opened. Gradually the light makes an impression on the film. The image appears. But it takes time.

It is the opposite of the way Job handled his despair.
He would not be patient. He would not take the time to
imagine God, to let God make an image on the film of his
life.

> What is my strength, that I should wait?
>   And what is my end, that I should be
>   patient?
> Is my strength the strength of stones *[he asks
>   sarcastically]*,
>   or is my flesh bronze? (Job 6:11,12).

> "Be still before the Lord," writes the psalmist,
> "and wait patiently for [God]" (Ps. 37:7).

The church are the people who wait with us in our
despair. It is virtually impossible to be patient alone, to
endure alone. The church are the people who call, who

arrive at the front door. It is no accident that Paul's great statement about hope's being produced by patience was made to a church. They had been patient with him. They had endured with him, even when he had persecuted them.

III

Hope begins in despair. It continues in patience. It is also grounded in reality. Hope is one way reality breaks through to us. It is one way we experience God. It is a process which goes all the way back in time, which, as we have suggested, means it goes all the way back in us. "Zeus gave [humanity] a vessel full of good things," reads an ancient fable of hope, "but [humanity], filled with curiosity, lifted the lid, so that all good things escaped to the gods, and when the lid was put back only [hope] was trapped, [humanity's] present comfort."[6]

"Faith," says the writer to the Hebrews, "is the assurance of things hoped for" (Heb. 11:1). "Assurance" was the Greek word "hypostasis," and it meant reality, what is substantial, actual, hypostatic rather than hypothetic. We move from hypothesis to hypostasis through the experience of our negative emotions. God becomes real as we become realized. Faith thus becomes, in the words of a biblical scholar, "the subjective appropriation of the objective hope."[7]

Perhaps a better way to put it is in terms of an image, because then we can see it. Remember, we are made in the image of God (see Gen. 1:27), and imagination is the way we "see" God. Hope is the "anchor of the soul" (Heb. 6:19). Whenever you see an anchor on a grave it is a sign of hope. When the anchor is in the water we do not see it, but we are held by it. We are anchored to the reality of God. The picture that is taken in the time exposure is of our frail craft riding the waves in the dead of night, buffeted by the storms of life which leave us desperate, but riding out the storms anchored to God.

When you see the anchors on the walls of the catacombs it makes you think. Did people die for an illusion? Or did they die for something that was so real to them in their despair that they would be willing to die for it? That reality is announced in the Old Testament, where what is hoped *for* is less frequently mentioned than the *basis* of hope, namely God.[8] And it continues to be announced in the New, where there are no adjectives or adverbs made out of the word for hope "because the accent," we are told, "does not fall on subjective feelings . . . but on the objective alignment of forces determining the human situation."[9]

Here's how the realist Paul puts it. It is how he realizes the presence of God. "Through [Christ] we have obtained access to this grace in which we stand, and we rejoice in our hope of sharing the glory of God" (Rom. 5:2). It is then that he talks about rejoicing in suffering because suffering produces patience and patience produces hope. Here's how it is expressed in another letter:

> [God] . . . saved us . . . so that we might be justified by . . . grace and become heirs in hope of eternal life. The saying is sure (Titus 3:5,7,8).

Here's how the realist Peter puts it, at the desperate time of the Neronian persecutions:

> By [God's] great mercy we have been born

> anew to a living hope through the resurrection
> of Jesus Christ from the dead . . . . In this you
> rejoice, though now . . . your faith . . . is tested
> by fire (1 Pet. 1:3,6,7).

The best proof of the resurrection, it has been argued, is the existence of the Christian Church. The early Christians were able to ride out the fire storm because they were anchored in reality.

IV

Perhaps the word we are groping for in our despair is not only reality but serenity. Hope gives serenity, or it is not hope. In our despair, we are anything but serene, but in our desperate patience, serenity comes. At least it can, as we get more and more in touch with reality. As reality, through our despair, gets more and more in touch with us, giving us its gift, serenity.

Who is the most serene person in your life? I'll wager it is the person who has been through the most, whose negative emotions have plunged him or her into repeated despair. Such people mediate the reality of God to us. They are demonstrating the new life Peter and Paul were writing about. "Since we have such a hope," Paul wrote, "we are very bold" (2 Cor. 3:12). Confident. Serene. "Cast all your anxieties on [God]," Peter wrote, "for [God] cares about you" (1 Pet. 5:7). Hope frees us from worry, the opposite of faith. Hope "binds" us "back" to the rest of who we are. But hope begins in despair.

Serenity is the opposite of complacency. Complacency relies on self. Serenity relies on God. Complacency says, "I am the master of my fate. I am the captain of my soul."[10]

Serenity says, "Behold, God is my salvation . . . the Lord God is my strength and my song" (Isa. 12:2). Complacency is lost in despair. Serenity begins in despair, as when your child has died. Then the words come across your despair, "Little girl . . . arise" (Mark 5:41). As an ancient realist put it, serene in his despair as he is patiently touched by reality:

> Blessed [are you] who [trust] in the Lord,
>   whose trust is the Lord.
> [You are] like a tree planted by water,
>   that sends out its roots by the stream,
> and does not fear when heat comes,
>   for its leaves remain green,
> and is not anxious in the year of drought,
>   for it does not cease to bear fruit (Jer. 17:7,8).

When you hit rock bottom, you hit rock. Or, as another ancient realist wrote:

> I will give you the treasures of darkness
>   and the hoards in secret places,
> that you may know that it is I, the Lord,
> the God of Israel, who call you by your
>   name (Isa 45:3).

Notes
1. Quoted by W. Kaufmann, *The Faith of a Heretic* (New York: Doubleday Anchor, 1961), p. vii.
2. Ibid., p. 94.
3. W. Barclay, *New Testament Words* (London: SCM, 1964), p. 143.
4. Idem.
5. Ibid., p. 145.

6. R. Bultmann in G. Kittel, *Theological Dictionary of the New Testament* (Grand Rapids, MI.: Eerdmans, 1964), vol. 2, p. 519.
7. P.S. Minear in *The Interpreter's Dictionary of the Bible* (New York: Abingdon, 1962), vol., 2, p. 643.
8. R. Bultmann, op. cit., p. 523.
9. P.S. Minear, op. cit., p. 641.
10. W. Henley, "Invictus."

EPILOGUE

The light shines in the darkness,
and the darkness has not overcome it.

John 1:5